Unstoppable in Stilettos

Unstoppable in Stilettos

A Girl's Guide to Living Tall in a Small World

Lauren Ruotolo

Health Communications, Inc.
Deerfield Beach, Florida

www.hcibooks.com

Library of Congress Cataloging-in-Publication Data

Ruotolo, Lauren.
　　Unstoppable in stilettos : a girl's guide to living tall in a small world /
Lauren Ruotolo.
　　　　p. cm.
　　　ISBN-13: 978-0-7573-1514-5
　　　ISBN-10: 0-7573-1514-3
　　　1. Ruotolo, Lauren.　2. Short people—United States—Biography.
3. Women—United States—Biography.　4. Stature, Short—Social
aspects—United States.　5. Short people—United States—Conduct of
life.　6. Women—United States—Conduct of life.　7. Success.
8. Optimism.　9. Self-esteem.　10. New York (N.Y.)—Biography.
I. Title.
CT275.R8753A3 2010
920.72—dc22
　　　　　　　　　　　　　　　　　　　　　　　　　　　　　2010035362

HCI, its logos, and marks are trademarks of Health Communications, Inc.

Publisher: Health Communications, Inc.
　　　　　　3201 S.W. 15th Street
　　　　　　Deerfield Beach, FL 33442–8190

Photography by Nelson Aguirre
Cover design by Larissa Hise Henoch
Interior design by Lawna Patterson Oldfield
Interior formatting by Dawn Von Strolley Grove

To my family,
who, every day, offers me
more happiness and strength.
I love you!

Life must be lived and curiosity kept alive.
One must never, for whatever reason, turn his back on life.

—ELEANOR ROOSEVELT

Hope lies in dreams, in one's imagination,
and in the courage of those
who dare to make dreams into reality.

—JONAS SALK

CONTENTS

INTRODUCTION

I hate to see people defeated. It's one of my biggest pet peeves. What's worse is when I see people giving in to defeat or being defeatist. It drives me completely insane! I don't understand it, and I want to immediately slap the silliness and insecurities out of someone who can actually look at me with a straight face and tell me that they "can't." Life should be lived large every day, and letting little obstacles get in the way and define who you are, even dictating the very circumstances that surround you, is no way to live. Don't get me wrong—I'm not trying to be your psychologist or pretending to be the expert on how to live, but if there is one thing I am sure to be mindful about, it's avoiding those little moments of defeat.

I'm thirty-four(ish) now, and I've finally gotten it through my thick skull that there's no time to shortchange yourself on the fun to be had, friends to be made, beauty to behold, ladders to climb, cocktails to shake, or stilettos to strut your stuff in. Defeat is an impediment to all these luxuries life has to offer. Yes, there are hindrances that can undo the driest martinis, make the highest Manolos appear out of reach, and, well, just generally complicate the best-laid plans. (Do I have to list 'em? Uncooperative boyfriends, pesky coworkers, Sunday drivers [aka slow drivers in the fast lane], stubborn hair, weight fluctuations, a rare medical condition . . . stop me when you've heard enough.) However, giving your encounters with the unfortunate the power to sidetrack you, make you second-guess yourself, or even hate—or God forbid, regret— the life you have, well, there's just no excuse for that. It's easier to be fearful than to be fearless (I made that one up myself!), and that's why I opt for taking the difficult way out—"fearless" is my middle name. But I haven't always been this way.

I remember very clearly what it's like to feel like I'm waffling through life, to be unsure of the decisions I am making. So many choices are in front of you on a daily basis, and lacking the experience or the gumption to know which one to make is enough to turn your tail upside down. Then there are the people we encounter—our bosses, new friends, old friends, family members, coworkers, men, women, drivers in the next lane who make us rage . . . the list goes on! Who can you trust, what's their purpose in your life, and how are they benefiting your life, and vice versa? More questions we must face! It's all the self-perpetuating drama of being a woman. We have the world at our feet, but sometimes we don't know where to step first!

Well, ladies, I've got a butt-kicking, far-reaching, all-encompassing, "good-for-me" plan that will make all obstacles seem like gum on the sidewalk: a little sticky, but nothing you can't walk around or over without getting your heels gooey.

Unstoppable in Stilettos is my homage to the good life, a unique strategy for having fun and doing well, which I arrived at very scientifically: by becoming an expert on being me. Okay, let me get something out of the way so we can get to the good part of my message to women. I was born with McCune-Albright syndrome, the clinical details of which are immaterial to my story except for the fact that this genetic blip has made me shorter than your average petite girl (I'm four feet two inches in flats, which I would never be caught dead in anyway). As a result of my size, I see the world from a unique angle—upward facing! And I happen to think it's a pretty good position to be in.

Oh, and did I mention the fact that doctors told me I'd be in a wheelchair for my entire life? Never happened. Not only can I walk, I do so in the highest possible heels. (More on that in Chapter 1.) Hey, I've even made it into the annals of the *New England Journal of Medicine*! Okay, there are a few more medical matters my condition presents aside from my stature, most of which are quite useful as metaphors for the purposes of this book: to help you become the person you want to be.

If you're thinking, "Well, I'm not short, I'm not the subject of a study in a medical journal, so what does this have to do with me?" I've got a news flash. Every one of us has got something that we think is stopping us from catching the brass ring, meeting Mr. Right, having our own reality show, or earning enough to buy what we want and save the world too—or claiming whatever it is we dream about. There is a little defeatist in everyone, and I am here to help pound it out of you. You can make use of what I've learned—about people, success, happiness, obstacles, and having a good time—to overcome whatever you believe is keeping you from achieving your goals.

Unstoppable in Stilettos shows, in eight inspirational, instructional, and memoiresque chapters that will have you rolling in the aisles and crying in the bathroom (the only acceptable place for a lady to weep), how to:

- ◆ Embrace your differences with zeal and good humor
- ◆ Deal with the quirks and craziness of other people without letting them get you down
- ◆ Overcome obstacles and get over your self-proclaimed flaws (they're actually assets!)
- ◆ Ignore "no" when it does not serve your purpose, and turn negativity on its head

- Conquer fear and overcome the dark times (no one is exempt from the "scary-sads"; you just can't let them take over)
- Embrace rejection and avoid the easy way out
- Find self-acceptance and take chances despite insecurities
- Beat insecurities, especially when it comes to meeting men (I have my own personal dating breakthrough story to share.)

I know, I know, you think you've heard it all before. You haven't! Second-guessing and negative self-talk are two of human nature's biggest curses. I should know: I was the queen of my own personal inquisition. As I said, I hate to see people defeated, to feel bad about themselves—especially women. When I know it is fear that is keeping them from reaching their potential, I turn into Lauren the Conqueror, ready to help slap fear or apathy in the face and take it down like the enemy it is. Through the examples I offer from my own life, I hope you will not only discover your hidden potential, but also find the best way to go after it and actually make your wildest dreams come true. Trust me—you will laugh, maybe shed a tear, but overall you will feel good about yourself by the end of this book.

My editor once asked me why I felt the need to write this book, what I wanted to share about my experiences, and how my life makes me equipped to offer inspiration to women who would like to receive it. Basically, she so tactfully asked me, "What the hell makes *you* so special, Lauren?" Good question. I thought about this and came to the conclusion that perhaps I could be the one to inspire you on how to avoid defeat, erase fear, and reach for your potential, because for my entire life I have had to chase down my own potential. I had to fight for my right to manifest my own destiny more than any other person I know. (And I have had—and continue to have—many more people than you can imagine tell me I can't.) Perhaps being a five-year-old who is told she can't run and play or a college graduate being considered "not quite the right match for our needs" after five-gazillion job interviews ignited something in me; something that makes me want to scream to naysayers "Bullshit!" I am living proof that it is.

While my physical growth has been stunted, it has been an ironic catalyst for my ability to flourish. And I love irony, as you may have noticed from the subtitle of this book. Why not share a little of the wealth and offer a proverbial tree branch to help pull you out of the quicksand of love, career, self, spirit, and relationships? Hey, don't worry! Aside from the heavy stuff, you'll also glean some knowledge on how to get to the front of any line (whether at the supermarket, airport security, or the hottest celeb hangout), triumph over naysayers, open a wine bottle on the beach with a crutch (problem-solving abilities have many benefits), create the dream job you've always wanted, and feel pretty all the time, among other essential skills.

So slip on your four- to six-inch stilettos, grab your biggest bag, and for goodness' sake put on a little lipstick, or at least some gloss, and some mascara (to bring out your eyes, darling!). We've got places to go, people to see, and lessons to learn.

1

A Course
in Obstacles

Lauren's Lesson:
It's not how many steps
are in front of you,
it's how you climb them

Seventy-five steep white concrete steps separate me from my hotel room in Santorini, Greece. I know because I counted them. But the motivation to descend each step down the cliff, where the hotel is nestled, makes the challenge worth it: my two favorite boys Cameron and Mikey and the promise of sharing with them a glass (or two or three) of crisp Greek white wine (which is similar to a sauvignon blanc) on the balcony of our honeymoon suite while watching the sunset hit the horizon of the vast Mediterranean. I cannot believe we have the honeymoon suite for the three of us. I am sure when we all checked in there were quiet snickers and confusion among the staff. By the way, it is not the traditional honeymoon suite that you would think of, but a regular room with angels on the walls.

Cameron and Mikey cheer me on from the bottom of the

cliff, as I descend mindfully one step at a time. "Go Shorty, you got it, work those muscles!" Right crutch. Right leg. Left foot. Left crutch. The way in which I use my silver and gray crutches to maneuver myself down the stairs is all very mechanically choreographed. It's a hike, and in my usual fashion, I make jokes and bitch along the way.

One staircase down and two to go. The last set is by far the scariest because it is shallow and spiral, a climactic ending to an already arduous trip. Each time this trip requires me to ascend and descend this threatening staircase, my nerves get the better of me and I never cease to be afraid. Each time I envision myself falling head-first. As I reach the final stair I see Mikey and Cameron waiting for me at the foot, which signals my nerves to cool off a bit. As I have done every time before, I reach the bottom again without a sweat and kick off my dusty shoes.

" It isn't necessarily the wine or the view, but the moment, shared with friends. "

When we finally get to the white and blue room, which is shaped like a dome and adorned with the aforementioned floating wedding angels that we sleep beneath in two beds atop gray concrete floors, my first stop is the small white refrigerator in the kitchen area. Waiting there is a bottle of the local Santorini white wine. Greeks are well known for their local wine and usually only serve it from within the particular region where the grapes were harvested. I call Cameron to come in and help me bring the glasses and chilled wine onto our balcony overlooking the sea and South Aegean Volcanic Arc. I pour some wine for the three of us into what I personally consider to be inappropriately small wineglasses that the hotel provided, so naturally I am compelled to fill them to the brim. What motivated me to make the steps also becomes my reward as well as a reminder of how wonderful my life is. It isn't necessarily the wine or the view, but the moment, shared with friends—a moment that I didn't miss out on because of my condition. A choice I consciously make on a daily basis and have been making since I was a little girl. You have one life to live and must live it to its fullest potential, condition or no condition.

We laugh, listen to, and dance to our summer mix on Cameron's iPhone, which includes lots of Lady GaGa and the new Madonna album, plus we take a million pictures of the sunset, the volcano, and Mikey. By the way, Mikey is our local New York weatherman, and he loves to take photos of himself and place them on Twitter for all his fans to see. Most of them are with his shirt off to showcase his hard-earned six-pack and oversized, muscular, chiseled chest. After two bottles of wine (hey, a reward is a reward!), we shower and get ready to make our way back up those seventy-five steps (even the steep, spirally ones) to town for dinner and drinks. My pleasant preparty warm-up primed me to retrace the journey. When I typically walk up stairs, I mainly use my upper body to stabilize myself on my crutches. This forces my upper body to work twice as hard as my lower body. So when I reach the final step back up the mountain, I am a bit out of breath and my bicep muscles feel as solid as rock. As I huff and puff, I say to myself, *Wow, I cannot believe I did this again.* I shout out to the boys in my Long Island accent, which deepens as I get more and more out of breath, "I hope the wine and grilled octopus is not too far away. That cab better be close by!" They just laugh and answer, "Shorty, keep hustling and that little ass moving."

> " Wearing impractical (but highly fashionable) stiletto heels is one of the ways I choose to tackle my obstacles. "

I cannot believe that I climbed up and down those seventy-five stairs at least four times a day, traveled through three islands, and walked through the Parthenon, all in a matter of a six-day Greek excursion. (Walking through the Parthenon is another story in itself with all the potholes and hills.) And it's no surprise to you, I'm sure, when I tell you that going up is twice as difficult as going down, but just like going down, going up brings another spectacular view, and of course another adventure into the beautiful and amazing Santorini night.

I feel unstoppable and ready for the evening in my signature Greek, white, four-inch Michael Kors wood-sole platform shoes. Donning a new white baby-doll sundress with long cotton and lace bell-bottom sleeves, my hair is in a slick ponytail with my bangs blown straight as a pin. I do not mind pulling my hair back, but I always blow out my bangs to disguise my long forehead. (Hairdressing hint: if you have a long forehead, cut bangs—and always blow them out, or it defeats the purpose.)

Santorini, of course, is a tourist destination, so it's interesting to witness the universal stares and cheers of onlookers. Every time I go up or down the cliff, someone watches me and says, "Wow, you're a trooper, how do you do it?!" But I'm not a trooper; it's how I live my life on a daily basis—facing mountainous climbs, subway entrances, the crosswalks and sidewalks of New York City—always aware of the number of steps, always foreseeing and planning for the obstacles, and always in stilettos.

"Okay, so what's with the heels, already?" you ask. How much can someone really love stilettos that they'd go as far as including the word in the title of her book? Well, wearing impractical (but highly fashionable) stiletto heels is one of the ways I choose to tackle my obstacles. It's become almost a signature of mine: the little girl with the big voice wearing the high heels. It's a description I've been hearing all my life, usually overheard from people left in a little cloud of dust as I careen past them toward my goal—whether that be an adorable pair of black patent leather five-inch cork platform shoes at Nordstrom, an A-list celebrity sitting poolside at an L.A. hotspot, or a yellow light to be beat from behind the wheel of my white Audi TT convertible.

" **Shoes have always been a way that I can express myself as a person who is in control.** "

Shoes have always been a way that I can express myself as a person who is in control. Everyone from my doctors and physical therapist to my parents told me I had to wear suitable shoes such as high-top sneakers and/or orthopedic shoes to help me walk. They told me that walking in anything else would cause me to feel unstable and that I could possibly break a leg. When I asked one doctor what constituted suitable, he suggested that I have shoes made "especially for you, as your right leg is almost two inches longer than the left."

I almost gagged when I saw the options. They

looked like granny shoes. And, since it's my nature to question explanations that make little or no sense or that have little or no precedence, I didn't let this opportunity slip by, so I inquired: How could wearing heels make me fall and break a leg when I wore nothing but sandals, slippers, and sneakers until I was ten years old, and still managed to break my hip seven times by the time I was eight? It's simple logic, people! At this point I was thirteen and was doing well, and what everyone, including the doctor, was saying about all things suitable didn't jive with my history. Did they really think I was out of my league? Or was it that everyone was scared and had no faith in me? I believe the main issue was that they had no faith in my disease. It is such a rare disease; how could anyone, even specialists, do anything other than suspect or generalize and play the "safe" card? But I was the one living with this condition, and therefore, I was the one who knew my limitations and knew if something made me feel good or not. I reasoned that if I was able to put one foot in front of the other, then it didn't matter how high the heel or how unsuitable the shoe (or how low the heel and how suitable the shoe).

As I have already mentioned, I was born with the somewhat mysterious and rare McCune-Albright syndrome. Researchers say it occurs in anywhere between 1 in 100,000 and 1 in 1 million people. Some people with the condition have short legs due to deformities (I do), have hormonal imbalances (yippee), and their bones can be easily broken and bruised (count me in), and therefore, they tend to go the wheelchair route to prevent brittle bones from continually breaking. That was never going to be a road I wanted to travel. (I'm much more comfortable on West Broadway in Soho or on the Long Island Expressway.) When I was just five years old I told my physical therapist, Carolyn, that I would never need a wheelchair. I was determined to walk despite the fact that the so-called "experts" told me otherwise. So far, so good!

Unlike people who are diagnosed with a challenging condition later in their lives, or those who fall victim to an unfortunate accident that impairs abilities they have grown accustomed to, my situation has been with me from the time I was just nine months old. Yet I have never let it define me. Perhaps that's why I never wanted to be treated like a "handicapped" or "challenged" person. I don't particularly feel like one. It's everyone else who seems to think there's something "wrong" with me—and therein lies the crux of my story. Through my

> ❝ I want to teach everyone who's ever felt tired of being pigeonholed and limited by other people's labels that they can do just about anything they want to. ❞

example, I want to teach everyone who's ever felt tired of being pigeonholed and limited by other people's labels that they can do just about anything they want to. If my life, times, and adventures don't prove that truism, I don't know what will convince the doubters out there.

So that's why I decided to begin this book with a lesson about obstacles and, ultimately, about the attitude you take on as you face them, because I was born into one giant obstacle. The secret to my success of climbing stairs, proverbial or not, is a five-prong effort:

1. **Always count them, which for you translates into knowing what's ahead of you, by being prepared.** If you are as knowledgeable as possible about the obstacle that you are about to tackle, you won't be caught too off guard and therefore will be much better equipped to make it through unscathed (and better for it) as a result.

2. **Accept your limitations as you make your climb.** Frankly, if I had climbed those steps in Santorini comparing myself to Cameron and Mikey as they waited for me at the top or bottom, or to any other tourist rushing down to view the cliff's picturesque edge, I would have felt solemn and defeated and been likely to give up. Comparing yourself to others is one giant waste of time. It won't change your climb, but it will most definitely make it unnecessarily longer and harder.

3. **Take one step at a time.** Yes, it's cliché, but for me, it's

literal. I take my time, step-by-step, unapologetic about my pace. Be mindful about your own steps, and never rush them or think you should be going faster. The pace you set for yourself is something to be proud of and will ultimately be responsible for your success.

4. **Reward yourself for your achievements or little attempts at achievement.** I am worth a glass of wine (or even two . . . who's counting?) at the end of seventy-five steps or a pair of new Marc Jacobs after a tiresome business trip. Rewarding yourself is a dignified way of acknowledging your efforts—of giving yourself a personal wink and a nod. You would do it for a friend or a colleague, so why not start with yourself?

It's not how many steps that are in front of you, it's how you climb them.

5. **Take on the obstacle your way.** I choose to walk around on crutches in stiletto heels. Why? 'Cause stilettos not only make me feel taller and more balanced, but offer me the satisfaction of knowing who I am and what I can accomplish. Wearing those heels reminds me that I call the shots and that ultimately I know what is truly suitable for me. Not

doctors. Not physical therapists. Not parents. Nobody but me. Sure, it may be easier for me to get around in sneakers or Naturalizers (God forbid!), but I feel powerful and unstoppable in stilettos.

And attitude is everything. You could implement one through four of this five-prong approach, but without five, you could just forget it. Basically, it's not how many steps that are in front of you, it's how you climb them.

What makes you feel unstoppable? Climb and find out!

2

AVOIDING LABELS AND OTHER PEOPLE'S INTERPRETATIONS OF YOU; OR, BE PREPARED TO FIGHT TO DEFINE YOURSELF

LAUREN'S LESSON:
LABELS ARE GREAT FOR FASHION BUT ARE TOTALLY GAUCHE WHEN USED ON PEOPLE

Don't get me wrong. I'm not this "shiny, happy person" every day. But a lot of my positive attitude and outlook on living is a personal choice that stems from a deep understanding of who I am and what I want out of life, which I recognized at a very early age. I was destined to be four feet two and walk with crutches, but with that destiny comes many difficult scenarios that require my making complicated choices and unconventional decisions. The first being: How will I choose to perceive my situation? Many people have philosophies on living, and this was my opportunity to discover my own. My philosophy: positivity! Oh, sometimes it's so easy to just be negative, to give in to the suckiness of it all, and wave the little white flag. But because it's in my power to choose to be positive or negative, I couldn't choose the latter. It's just not in me. And besides, what would that do to my power? To be negative would be the number one and quickest way to validate so many of the labels that people feel compelled to put upon me, like the label of victim. That's one I've been fighting all my life, and the choice of positivity has helped remove that label and change the perception that I have of myself and that others have of me. Since I choose to see my real self as a capable and gifted person who can conquer anything, others see me for that as well, instead of as a victim of a genetic lottery gone bad.

Labels are one of my favorite topics, especially in fashion, where labels are actually much better suited than on people—identifying someone as "something" or placing them in a group category that reeks of judgment and hypocrisy is just plain gauche. It's human nature to do it, and I suspect we picked it up as children from the cues we received from adults who acted like high-school kids, or in grade school when we realized the girls who liked to read got the least attention from the boys. But for me, the key to avoiding labels has been the possession of a keen sense of how to define myself,

> " The key to avoiding labels has been the possession of a keen sense of how to define myself. "

which I was able to recognize by the time I was about five years old. I realize it is rare to be so young and so in tune with what feels foreign and what feels right, and I tend to believe that this ability was a biological gift; a part of my disease, to help me get through it and beat it in every way possible. I also believe that nurture is responsible too, as I have two of the best parents anyone could ever have, who cultivated me and allowed me to experience myself through my own eyes and nobody else's.

Speaking of the parents: In June 1976, I was born to George and Holly, who had recently moved from their small 1970s-motif one-bedroom apartment in Mineola, New York—a bustling little Long Island town about forty minutes outside of New York City—to a cozy neighborhood known as Huntington Hills in Dix Hills, New York, the epitome of suburbia. There were three different kinds of homes on my block: the standard colonial with tons of trees in the front yard, which almost covered the view of the house from the street; the larger colonial with an extremely steep driveway; and then the house that my parents bought—a ranch with an acre of property. For a couple who lived comfortably and humbly in small spaces, this move was the fruition of all their grandiose dreams and goals combined. My parents were alone in that house for exactly one year until I came along on the day they celebrated their fifth wedding anniversary. (And they say wood is the traditional fifth-year anniversary gift!) After eighteen hours of labor and pushing that ultimately led to my mother having a C-section, I was born, weighing six pounds, fourteen ounces, a perfect little baby girl with a cone head. (Thanks to my big egg getting stuck in the birth canal—sorry, Mom!)

I was pretty easy for a first child. Eat and sleep, eat and sleep. That's what I did pretty steadily with a few crying bouts that could be muted by putting a bottle into my mouth. (Today I am not much different; you can put a great bowl of pasta with marinara—I call it red sauce—and a glass of Malbec in front of me, and I am happy.)

Things were moving according to plan and for nine months I was a happy and healthy baby. And then I got my period. Yes, you read that correctly. At nine months of age, my body unleashed its adolescent call. When other people tell you they grew up fast, they often mean by adolescence, they were smoking cigarettes and drinking Jack Daniels or holding down two jobs to help feed their family. I had them beat by more than a decade!

> " My pediatrician was astonished at what my mother told him. "

My pediatrician was astonished at what my mother told him and sent me to a specialist who told my mother that it looked as if diaper pins had gotten lost inside of me, because I was always bleeding. By the way, it was 1977, not 1956, and my mother used Pampers, not cotton diapers and safety pins. So, with no answers and knowing something was seriously wrong, my mother took me to another specialist, this time a competent, expert pediatric endocrinologist named Dr. Platon Collipp. He was the first doctor to tell my parents that he had seen accelerated growth or "precocious puberty" in other young patients, and this was something he wanted to monitor. He wanted to see me at least once a month and to take blood work over the next year. I was immediately put on Depo-Provera, a hormone that put a stop to my precocious puberty, as well as Inderal, which was prescribed to me experimentally. It lowers the heart rate and is normally used in patients with heart problems, but was given to me to slow down my pituitary gland—the master gland of the endocrine system (the system of hormones). As if that wasn't complicated enough, I began experiencing seizures, which were deemed unassociated with my precocious puberty, but frustratingly had no known cause. The seizures occurred about twice a week and the doctors were confident that medication would arrest them, so I was prescribed phenobarbital, a barbiturate drug with a sedative and hypnotic effect on the central nervous system. My mother was told to administer this pill at bedtime, unlike the other drugs. The seizures only lasted a year and subsided by my second birthday, but combined with everything else, this was another blow to me and my family.

The next few months and years were extremely challenging for my parents. I was so young that I could not understand, and to this day I really don't remember quite what happened. But for my mother and father, at only twenty-six and thirty-one, respectively, it was a huge struggle to adjust to the oddest and most unexpected circumstances after having a completely healthy baby for nine months. Even though I had hormonal issues and was prepubescent, I was crawling, walking, and was even potty trained by the time I was one year old.

> " My parents were plagued with guilt. . . . They felt scared, sometimes even terrified, and didn't know what to expect. "

For my first birthday my parents threw a huge celebration and even had a pony for me to ride on. Everything seemed to be okay again. Then after I turned two I was with my father at a pigeon store . . . yes, a pigeon store (his part-time hobby of raising pigeons has today turned into an 600-square-foot pigeon coop with more than 200 birds in my parents' backyard), and I slipped into a puddle of water. Not knowing exactly what was wrong or what to do, my father immediately took me home and put me down for a nap. When I woke up I was screaming and holding my leg, which by then was extremely swollen. He phoned my mother and told her what was going on. My father took me to Huntington Hospital where my mother met us, and I was exposed to rounds of routine x-rays. The doctors said I had a broken femur (for any of you who are not aspiring orthopedic surgeons, that's code for thighbone), but initially said nothing to my parents about what the x-rays further revealed. I was put into a body cast and admitted into the hospital for two days, and on the day I was released the doctors told my parents that something was seriously wrong; they had put together the precocious puberty symptoms with the cystic-looking bones they saw in the x-ray and diagnosed me with McCune-Albright syndrome. My parents were plagued with guilt. As first-time and inexperienced parents, they somehow felt responsible for my condition and vowed to find the best possible doctors to help me. They felt scared, sometimes even terrified, and didn't know what to expect. They continuously asked themselves, "Why did this have to happen to *our* child?"

My mother was the strong, tough parent from the beginning. She was extremely proactive and positive and made it her mission to try to eliminate any future problems the doctors might foresee. Both of my parents reached out to every one of their friends and family to gain access to the best possible doctors. However, my mother challenged many doctors, dissecting everything they said, and sometimes testing them on their knowledge of my disease to always make sure they were giving me appropriate treatment.

My father who was (and still is) a very positive man, processed the news of my diagnosis differently; he was extremely disturbed and very somber. He began to eliminate the small pleasures in his life, such as listening to the radio in the car, watching funny movies, and making jokes. His attitude was that if I was suffering, he should be suffering as well. Within a few weeks my father also started to attend church to pray for me. Church was very new to his routine, and he figured that if he prayed to God for me to be okay, then I would be. To this day he attends church every Sunday and prays for me and the rest of my family.

Today my father is my biggest advocate.

This was an extremely hard time for both of my parents and within a year of my diagnosis they started to see a therapist to work through their feelings. A marriage is definitely tested when children enter the picture, but having a child with a disease is an even bigger strain. But they got through the bad times and today my father is my biggest advocate. He is so proud, and actually brags about my achievements to everyone he meets. In June 2011 my parents will celebrate their fortieth wedding anniversary!

A few days after my diagnosis I was brought to Nassau County Medical Center where Dr. Collipp practiced, and he explained everything to my parents. There was a lot more involved in my condition than just precocious puberty and cystic bones. After reviewing my x-rays with my parents, Dr. Collipp combined my history of hormonal imbalances along with my cystic bones, which is technically called polyostotic fibrous dysplasia, and reconfirmed the diagnosis of McCune-Albright syndrome.

McCune-Albright syndrome is a genetic disorder of the skeletal system that creates hormonal problems along with premature puberty, and is caused by mutations in the GNAS1 gene. The abnormal gene is present in a fraction, but not all, of the patient's cells. This disease is not inherited; it is caused by a new change (mutation) to the deoxyribonucleic acid (DNA) that occurs in the womb while the fetus is developing. This mutation has never been passed on to subsequent offspring. Sometimes my condition is called an "orphan disease," because it is too rare for pharmaceutical companies to "adopt" it for research and drug development. Basically, there aren't enough people who have it, so how can companies make money on the medication? Couple the fact that there weren't a lot of medical personnel who were treating me who had direct experience with McCune-Albright (named for Donovan James McCune and Fuller Albright, who first described the disease in 1937, for any Wikipedia fans out there) with the raging hormonal changes I was experiencing, and you get a recipe for some fairly annoying physical and emotional explosions.

About a week after the removal of the body cast, I fractured my left femur. I was in a lot of pain and my parents were in awe. They were told I had cystic bones and that it's one of the identifying traits of my disease, but the fact that I broke it by simply turning over in my sleep was just baffling. And so soon after my body cast was off, well, the gravitas of it all really set it. I was just a two-year-old baby, and all of this was happening at a stunning pace.

> " When it comes to your health and medical matters, don't ever assume that everyone is on the same page. "

The doctors recommended the left femur be surgically repaired to help correct what they called a Shepherd's crook deformity (which makes the bone look similar to a question mark); then they recommended an osteotomy (breaking the bone and resetting it the way they want it to heal). The three-hour surgery was going to be performed a few hours later at Nassau County Medical Center, conducted by Dr. John Handelsman (head of pediatric orthopedics) who had worked with Dr. Collipp in the past. My parents were signing off on all the paperwork when the anesthesiologist came in to introduce himself. My father mentioned that I was taking Inderal.

According to my father, the anesthesiologist's face turned completely white and he ran out of the room and immediately canceled and rescheduled the surgery for the next day.

Because one of the functions of Inderal is to slow the heart rate, an anesthesiologist unknowingly putting me under while the Inderal was in my system could have been deadly. My father saved my life by telling the doctor about my medications, as patients on this particular drug need to have different drugs and tests administered before surgery. If the surgery had been performed, I would not be writing this book today. A very important lesson was learned that day: when it comes to your health and medical matters, don't ever assume that everyone is on the same page, has the same information, is asking the most thorough questions, or knows as much as you do about your medical history.

I gave new meaning to the "terrible twos," as I lived most of them in full-body casts while in and out of the hospital more times than I could count before the age of five. That was when my mother became pregnant with my sister Addy, and the pressure of picking me up all the time hurt her back. To make life a little easier, my parents actually bought an ambulance stretcher until they could find a wheelchair that reclined, because it was easier for them to carry the stretcher than to carry me. My bones, particularly my hips, had been the most trouble, and to this day, every time I hear a saw, my heart instantly races and I get a little nervous. With all the miracles of modern medicine, a saw was all that was used to remove my body casts. You would think it would be a noise that I remember as joyful since my casts were coming off, but instead it catapults me back to doctors' offices and lying on a cold steel table under lights that were as bright as the Empire State Building and a pillow under my head for whatever comfort I could be offered. The nurses would come in first and prepare the room and then the doctor would arrive in his blue scrubs and they would remove my casts. The room would fill with dust and my leg would get hot and vibrate because of the speed of the saw. After the casts came off I felt weak and the hair on my leg was like a

> " The sound of a saw makes me feel like a scared little girl. It is my kryptonite. "

shaggy dog's. Put simply, the sound of a saw makes me feel like a scared little girl. It is my kryptonite.

After that, some pretty major developmental stages that take a lifetime in most people were, for me, condensed into a few years, and some pretty bizarre hormonal changes were happening inside of me. I had frequent emotional explosions since my hormone levels were always either extremely high or low. In fact, my estrogen levels sometimes went as high as 500 pg/ml (picograms—one-trillionth of a gram—per milliliter). Normal levels range from 50–400 pg/ml while a woman is having her menstrual cycle. Since I was not even ten years old, and the doctors stopped me from getting my period with the use of hormone replacement medications, my mood swings were undeniably hard for me. One day I would feel perfectly normal and the next day I could feel happy and sad in the same moment. Emotional roller coasters are hard enough to understand in adulthood, but at ten they were especially confusing, frustrating, and frightening.

And than I went through menopause at eleven. My estrogen levels became really high at that time, so the doctors put me on medicine that threw me into early menopause. I lost a lot of weight, became very moody, and had hot flashes—sometimes during a pop quiz in math class.

By the time I was eight years old, I had finished growing physically and had broken my hip seven times (with every break came more hip and leg deformities). Until that time I had always been the tallest kid in my class. Ironic, isn't it, given the fact that I'm just about four feet two inches tall, making me the shortest person in most places and rooms these days. Also during this time I started to develop and began getting breasts, and hair in my pubic area and under my armpits.

While I don't remember the pain and the casts and the surgeries of my earlier years, I have vivid recollections of when I began to develop in the summer I turned eight. I started to hide my body—and then myself—since I looked different from all the other girls in my camp. I was an eight-year-old who had small breasts, pubic hair, and zits. Trust me— it was not a good look, and I think all the pictures that were taken are hidden in my safe. At camp I was embarrassed since we had to change in front of everyone for swim class. For some semblance of privacy, I would change in the bathroom and try to hide the fact that my body looked more like a fifteen-year-old's than an eight-year-old little girl's.

Different was not something I thought of as a good thing when I was younger, so at the age

> " From that day forward I would take the long, hard road ahead of me rather than sit and let the world go by. "

of five I made a decision that I would stand by for the rest of my life. I decided to say *no* to a wheelchair and *yes* to walking. With so many deformities already present in both my femurs, the doctors felt a wheelchair was the safest and easiest route. It was clear that the doctors' philosophy was that another fracture was only a matter of time, so "play passive and stay seated before it can happen again." Neither my parents nor I agreed that I was best suited for life in a wheelchair, and they took me to another bone specialist who was recommended by a close family friend. Dr. John Siffert was a specialist in cystic bones and practiced at Mount Sinai hospital. He immediately looked at me and my x-rays, and agreed with the doctors about the risk; however, he believed that strengthening the muscles was necessary to keep the bones strong. Therefore, he prescribed physical therapy immediately, and my parents, never straying from their promise, were off on a search to find the best.

Many physical therapists took a look at me and my bones and straightaway labeled me as "fragile," refusing to take on the case. Finally, my parents met a physical therapist who referred us to the tougher-than-nails woman who would change my life with just her first knock on our front door. Carolyn (who is the most direct person I have ever met) asked me one question: "Lauren, do you want to walk?" Of course, the obvious answer for anyone would be *yes*, but to a five-year-old whose greatest priority was to be able to run with the rest of her friends, this decision was paramount, and one that molded me for life. From that day forward I would take the long, hard road ahead of me rather than sit and let the world go by. My answer was "*Yes*, and I say *no* to a wheelchair." Even at that young age the word "wheelchair" frightened me. I was an independent little girl who knew exactly where she was headed and was going to do her own walking—one foot in front of the other. I was already sensitive to labels and feared the label of "different," so it was important for me to work my hardest and do whatever was in my preschool-age power to avoid that label. If it was meant to be, so be it, but Carolyn's question led me to believe it was a battle of wills more than destiny knocking.

> In fact, the word *no* was completely removed from my vocabulary.

This decision to walk resulted in my working with Carolyn as my physical therapist for the next fifteen years. She became my second mother, my coach, my doctor, and my confidant. I saw her three to four days a week for at least thirty minutes, and no matter what exercise we did, I always had to do three sets of twenty. Most of the time each exercise required at least ten pounds of ankle weights on each leg. In the winter and colder months, we worked in my parents' basement where my dad built a minigym for me. In the summer, most of our workouts were either in the pool or down the driveway and onto the street. No matter what the temperature was outside, I was never allowed to say *no* to therapy. In fact, the word *no* was completely removed from my vocabulary.

On the days Carolyn wasn't at my house, I had to practice the exercises on my own. She expected me to do thirty to sixty minutes independently daily. This was added torture to a child; imagine having to do your schoolwork and then another hour of physical therapy. I'm not going to lie—like I did to Carolyn when I was a child. She would ask me if I had done at least thirty minutes on my own. I told her I had, but actually I'd only done maybe ten or fifteen minutes of the dreaded treadmill with five- to ten-pound weights on each leg. I hated the treadmill as much as I hated science class. Oh, and let me tell you that this was not the treadmill you walk on at your local gym. This was manual, so I had to make it run on my own. I hated it. I mean *hated* it! They say hard work has a big payoff. Well, in my case this is true, and physical therapy might have been exhausting and something I hated doing, but I was able to walk when I was five and still can to this day. Whether I am with or without crutches, I am vertical every day and love it.

Physical therapy might have held me back from doing after-school activities with the rest of my classmates, but I knew it was necessary to move me toward my goal. Everyone who was in my life knew about therapy and would come over to witness it; for some kids this was an adventure and they wanted to try it, while others just knew about it but were not as eager to come and experience it. No matter what, none of my friends ever made me feel different or put a label on me, even though I could not join the soccer or softball teams or the school play. It was always the parents who would attach a label to what I could and couldn't do. What really amazes me is that children view you for who you are, but adults are so quick to label you and put you in this basket that says there is something wrong with you.

> I felt an armor build around me that could resist the labels that others, mostly adults, thrust upon me.

The decision to go to any length to ensure I could walk molded me into the strong and independent woman I am today. The regimen Carolyn had me on, plus the independent exercise (notwithstanding secretly abbreviated sessions), taught me about self-discipline, sacrifice, and good old-fashioned sweat. With each day that I became stronger, I felt an armor build around me that could resist the labels that others, mostly adults, thrust upon me. It helped me see for myself who I really was, and how I wanted to present myself to the world as the hardworking, determined, gifted person I was.

The feeling that we all have when we accomplish something that people said or thought was impossible is more gratifying than any material thing we could reward ourselves with. Accomplishment is the best gift you can offer yourself, and that comes with knowing and accepting who you truly are and what you are capable of, no matter what people on the outside may opine about you. And I had to fight—hard—to define myself, whether it was in physical therapy, questioning doctors, or ignoring what my friends' parents thought about my capabilities. Sure, I was labeled "different" and "fragile," like I could break or something, which couldn't have been farther from the truth. Nothing about me is broken. They are the ones who are broken, not me.

The same is true for you! You may not have had to say to yourself, "To walk or not to walk, that is the question!" at the age of five, but I would bet my crutches that at some point in your life, perhaps even frequently, you've felt assessed, judged, misunderstood, or labeled. Unfortunately, it's unavoidable. I can talk to psychologists and sociologists who could give me a gazillion reasons why humans do this to each other. Is it a defense mechanism? Is it a response from feeling threatened? Is it projecting our own self-hatred? Do we just not have time to get to know anyone anymore, so labels provide a quick inventory on who is out there and whether or not they fit into our life? And the list goes on. We don't have the time or resources to determine the answers in this book, and we certainly can't stop the label game in its tracks, so I say we become proactive instead of reactive. First, acknowledge that labels are a sad fact of life, and second, know there are things we can do about them, such as:

1. If someone puts a label on you, consider that they are doing so to combat their own insecurities.

2. Sometimes a label is actually an asset as it may allow you to stand out in a crowd and let you shine. It's really all about how you work the label.

> " If someone puts a label on you, consider that they are doing so to combat their own insecurities. "

3. Two wrongs don't make a right. If you are labeled, avoid labeling back. You will just become petty and ignorant like the labeler. Take the high road.

4. Consider the source. Who is doing the labeling? Is it someone you need respect from? Have you just met the person? You ultimately know who understands you in life, and most likely those people have either been in your life along

time or they actually contribute something of value to your existence. Anyone who puts a label on you will be in and out of your life in a flash, so give as much of a flash of time's notice of it.

5. Be stoic and laugh it off. Sometimes laughing with people when they make an assumption or remark about you will catch them off guard and totally disarm them! It's fun to watch.

Don't ever buy into labels. Look, it's definitely easier to believe the bad stuff, and if you hear the same thing enough times, you can start to believe it. This is why it's very important to truly know who you are. Once you do, nobody can redefine you from the outside. That's the greatest MO of all.

3

Naysayers and Non-doers, and Why I Don't Associate with Them

Lauren's Lesson:
Avoid the word "no" at all costs

Have you ever thought about making a list of the people who tried to stop you from getting somewhere or accomplishing something, and a list of those who helped you achieve a goal? Consider doing this exercise so you can see, in black and white, just how many people try to get in your way when you are trying to get somewhere, and how many people are willing to give you a leg up. Funny thing is, even though the second list is probably shorter, one or two helping hands are so much more powerful than ten obstacle makers. There were always people, whether out of fear or ignorance, who tried to stop me. Believe me when I say it would have been all too easy for me to give in to them and sit at home. But my own tenacity, and the support of a few other people who were wonderfully help-ful, made the difference for me between having a very circumscribed life and leading what is a very full one. And the most powerful assistance in life is that which you give yourself (your name should be number one on the help list, and if it's not, you need to put it up there right now).

From the time I was diagnosed, my parents remained positive, and when the doctors told them, "No, she will never . . . " they turned a deaf ear to the statement and moved on. By definition, the word *no* is used to express refusal, denial, disbelief, emphasis, or disagreement. It's much easier to use the word *no* in any statement because *no* can equal laziness and can therefore stop you from your ultimate goals.

> " By definition, the word *no* is used to express refusal, denial, disbelief, emphasis, or disagreement. "

In the beginning, my parents were my voice and never let anyone tell them that I could not do something. From time to time people would try to give my parents advice on how to deal with my disability ("Well, Lauren can't [fill in the blank] so we would rather she not be around") or with them ("Lauren might find out about something she won't be able to do, so I did not want to upset her"). My parents said BS to all those excuses.

For instance, in second grade I was not invited to a roller-skate birthday party when my friend's mother determined that I would not attend because I could not skate. The birthday girl was a good friend of mine, and while all the other parents were scheduling to take their kids to the party, my mother intervened with this girl's parents. My parents knew how upset and out of place I'd feel if I was not invited, so my mother called and told the other mother, "I do not understand why you think Lauren cannot attend the party. She is very capable of knowing what she can and cannot do, and by the way, not all the kids will be roller-skating the entire time. She can participate in many of the other activities. Next time please call me before you make any decisions about my child."

Since finding my own voice at around ten, I have always created my own path and never allow anyone to tell me what I can and cannot do. I spent a lot of time proving my abilities to naysayers, just to show them they're wrong, but climbing stairs just to put people in their place is no reason to climb stairs. Doing it for me is so much more satisfying. And when I know I can do something, it means nothing to me whether or not an outsider feels the same. Fortunately for me, the word *no* is not in my vocabulary.

Perseverance is a skill that assists you in dealing with every *no* in life, in whatever form it may take. Courage is another. They go hand in hand, as it takes courage to persevere. But these are also skills that need time to form, like a muscle that needs to be broken down to build it up. I was fortunate enough to have many encounters that required perseverance and courage, and a most significant one when I was just twelve years old. It was an experience that strengthened my resolve to never let life get to me—and to never accept a bad haircut ever again! The story begins, though, when I was just four years old.

Walt Disney World and I do not mix. Without exception, something bad has happened every time I have gone there. The first time I experienced Disney World was when I was four years old. My grandmother, aka Nanny Bev, stayed with my younger sister Addy, who was only a baby at the time, while my parents and I went to Florida. One of my most vivid memories is of riding Space Mountain with my dad. Basically, Space Mountain is an indoor roller coaster that operates in pitch darkness. I remember screaming at the top of my lungs, frightened that I was going to have a heart attack. But it was one of those "it's so scary, it's fun" experiences, so in the end, I enjoyed the thrill. But we had to leave Disney World early because back at home, Addy ate animal poop she found on the ground in Nanny's backyard and

> " Walt Disney World and I do not mix. "

had to be hospitalized. Way to be a killjoy, Ad! The next time I went to Disney, it was with a broken ankle, thanks to an overturned snowmobile that landed on me. But, hey, three's a charm.

The third time I went off to the Magic Kingdom, it became a seminal part of a series of events that eventually made medical history. Our entire family made the trip this time, including an aunt and uncle, and my cousins Jenna and Jesse. We were on our way to Orlando for what, I was positive, would be a fantastic vacation with Mickey and Minnie. I was full of anticipation and optimism. I was thirteen and still riding the high of my bat mitzvah. I was looking forward not only to the impending trip to Florida, but also to the coming celebrations of my friends when I got back, especially Geoff Wasserman's. (His party was going to be in the city—exciting!—at a place called Private Eyes, which still exists and is now a gay bar, but I digress.)

Meanwhile, I had been having horrible headaches for two weeks prior to the trip. My left eye started tearing and would not stop. A visit to the school nurse reassured me that everything was fine; that I probably just had a cold. Another week passed and still the headaches and tearing continued. My mother took me to my pediatrician, who thought I had a sinus infection. He prescribed a combination of medicines to fight the infection, help the headaches, and stop the tearing. Despite this cornucopia of pharmacology, none of my symptoms were getting better.

I complained to my physical therapist, Carolyn, about my pain. It was getting so bad that my left eye was starting to protrude a bit, in what seemed to be protest. "You can't go to Disney World, Lauren" I remember her telling me as I was walking up from the basement steps. But I insisted that I'd be fine and I had to go. I was not going to be responsible for ruining my family's trip. By this time I'd gotten very good at putting up with the indignities and aches and pains that my condition sometimes presented. Besides, I'm not a complainer per se.

> " I'd gotten very good at putting up with the indignities and aches and pains. "

It's just that my head really did hurt! With her usual prescience, Carolyn told me, "You're going to be in the ER within twenty-four hours."

But off we went to Disney World. I kept insisting that I was fine, even though I was not fine at all. I was in incredible pain. My head felt as if a pound of bricks had been placed on top of it. My eye seemed to be jutting out even more. Adding insult to injury—literally—I had an ugly, short, curly bob haircut (which my dad had styled [thanks, Dad!]), and braces on my teeth. Okay, are you getting the picture? Oh, and did I mention my ankle was broken (again) and I was sporting a hot pink cast? Attractive!

So anyway, we were at the hotel and my head felt like it was about to break in two, so my mother called the hotel doctor, who confirmed that I seemed to have a really bad sinus infection. So why weren't the meds working? I was a mess. Of course, this did not stop me from having my picture taken with all the characters. (I look at those photographs now and simply cannot believe the person standing next to Goofy is yours truly.)

Just like the two previous trips to Florida, we went home early. I wasn't getting any better, and, in fact, my eye was becoming visibly worse. Carolyn said, "I told you so" when she saw me. She and my mom took me to Schneider Children's Hospital to get an MRI. Afterward, the radiologist, and not the neurosurgeon, told us that I had a cyst behind my eye that was causing pressure. That was what was causing my headaches, the protrusion of my eye, and its tearing. The cyst was a side effect of my disease, so it was all related.

Remember, I was thirteen. Naturally, I was terrified and I began crying. This is not what I wanted to hear from a radiologist who did not know anything about my condition. So the next stop was Manhattan to see one of the top pediatric neurosurgeons on the East Coast (who I will call Dr. Goodall). He confirmed that I did indeed have a large cyst behind my eye that needed to be removed. The procedure? A craniotomy, which is basically an operation that requires the surgeon to slice open your skull!

He emphasized that surgery had to be done right away because he feared infection. But there was a catch—even though Dr. Goodall thought the circumstances were dire, he asked us to schedule the procedure to be performed in three weeks, since he was going on vacation and would be out of town until then. That's when my mother walked out the door. Okay, now I really went over the edge. First of all, this seemed like a serious operation, and the guy wanted us to wait until he was back from Bermuda or wherever he was going? Plus, I'd miss Geoff Wasserman's bar mitzvah *and* my head would have to get shaved. Listen, I wanted to change my awful haircut, but I had something a lot less drastic in mind.

> " I wanted to change my awful haircut, but I had something a lot less drastic in mind. "

My mother insisted that a craniotomy was not the right way to go at this point. We needed a third opinion. Carolyn became my savior; her daughter, Karen, is a neurologist who specializes in epilepsy, and she recommended a top neurosurgeon at Johns Hopkins. Dr. Ben Carson was a pediatric neurosurgeon who would normally be impossible to get an appointment with, but

Karen was able to secure a time for us to see him. My mom, her sister (my aunt Robyn), and I were on a plane to Baltimore the next day. Since my parents own a hair salon, my dad had to stay behind (and call us ten times a day) so they could keep the business open.

We got to Johns Hopkins and sat in the waiting room, anticipating the arrival of the doctor. Finally, a very young (maybe thirty-six years old), small, black man wearing scrubs came in and started to ask us a lot of questions. I don't know if we were imagining Brad Pitt riding in on a stallion with stethoscope in hand, but it took us a while (since he never introduced himself) to figure out that this youthful, diminutive man in work clothes was Dr. Carson, and not an intern.

He might have been young but he was reported to be the best in his field. His recommendation? A craniotomy. All of a sudden it became clear to me—I would have to have this serious operation, have my head shaved, and miss Geoff Wasserman's bar mitzvah! Could life get any worse? Still, Dr. Carson had spoken to the other medical professionals at the hospital and everyone was in agreement, from the ophthalmologist to the ear, nose, and throat specialist (ENT) that surgery was necessary to remove the cyst and relieve the pressure on my eye. Since he too was worried about infection, the doctor admitted me right away, and the operation was scheduled for two days later.

At around 5 PM, the ENT, Dr. David Eisele (he was not

Brad Pitt, either, but came really close), paid a visit and explained to my mom and me that he wanted to try something before the operation. The cyst, which we had by now found out was benign, was right behind my sinuses, which was why my eye was protruding. He wanted to try endoscopic surgery, a brand-new procedure at the time. Since I had already been admitted to the hospital, it could be done right away.

He explained that the procedure would be less invasive than a craniotomy (that was an understatement; they wouldn't tear open my skull!). They would drain the cyst by inserting small tools through my nose to operate on it.

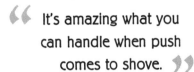

> It's amazing what you can handle when push comes to shove.

We were not afraid, and agreed to try the procedure, because it was clear that if the course of action did not work, it would not hurt me. The endoscopy would be easier than a craniotomy and there would be far less recovery time. I mean, I would still miss Geoff Wasserman's party, but at least they wouldn't have to shave my head. And by the way, the bad haircut became my favorite one—I loved saving my hair.

By 8 PM I was in the operating room and

about to undergo seven hours of surgery. That night the doctor literally popped the cyst and my eye slowly went back into its socket. The surgery was repeated three days later to make sure they got it all, and that second surgery only took about an hour. The following day I was released, but had to return to Baltimore every week for the first month. We continued to make that trip once a month for the next six months because my eye needed constant measuring and monitoring to see whether or not the cyst was growing back. Because it was the first time endoscopic surgery had been used to remove a cyst, I was written up in the *New England Journal of Medicine*. Hey, I was just trying to help out in any way that I could!

It's amazing what you can handle when push comes to shove. I cannot say what another person would have done in this situation—perhaps there are those who would have been afraid to go forward with an untried procedure. Maybe someone else would have thought her life was over because she was faced with a daunting prognosis. Not me. Never. There may be times when you are faced with a metaphorical or even a real craniotomy. Stay open. Be brave.

Courage came in handy again when I was about fourteen. You see, I thought I was the best singer in the world (or maybe it was just wishful thinking). Since I first began junior high school at age twelve, I was in the chorus and I tried out for all the school plays and musicals. It was springtime and we heard a rumor that rap star LL Cool J was moving to the neighborhood. I thought *OMG, this is my chance*, and

I was determined to meet him. On a chilly spring day, wearing my multicolor hot dogger (a running suit; obviously for fashion and not function) and white EG Smith socks (EGs were the coolest 1980s brand) scrunched down to my sneakers, my friend Samantha (who lived across the street) and I walked over to his house. It was about fifteen houses away, up a huge hill. We talked about how excited we were to meet him and hoped that he was home. By the time we entered his driveway, I was exhausted and my legs were very tired. Walking up and down a hilly street with crutches is a lot more difficult than you would think.

" I thought I was great and destined for the Top 40. "

We finally got to his house, which was a modern-looking white ranch, but it was the only house on the block that had a black iron gate around the entire property. Samantha and I rang the bell; a man answered the door. I asked if LL (which stands for Ladies Love, in case you are not down with your '80s rap) was home, and when he arrived at the door we welcomed him to the neighborhood and asked if he would listen to an "audition." While I didn't do much in the preparation department, like vocal lessons (or even warm-ups, for that matter), I did bake a cake. Where I come from, you don't show up to someone's home empty-handed.

The look on his face was very neighborly but I am sure he felt as awkward as I did. I remember being so nervous that I could not bolt out the Whitney Houston song "How Will I Know," which I had practiced in my room for hours. I tried to sing the chorus and got out the first two lines. Samantha just stood there and looked at me. LL was very gracious but turned down the chance to make me a singing sensation—go figure! I believe he thought I was a cute kid because he told me to practice and keep up the good work.

I insisted on taking singing lessons and wanted to get into advanced chorus. It's a wonder my family didn't need corrective ear surgery. I thought I was great and destined for the Top 40. No one could tell me otherwise. I was horrible; well, not *that* bad. And, eventually, I realized on my own that I was not going to be the next Madonna or Whitney Houston. But my decision to stop pursuing my dream of a singing career was on my terms and not anyone else's. I made the call in my own time, when I was ready to admit my shortcomings. But I found a way to channel my love for music by getting internships at radio stations and at MTV, and eventually I decided on a career in the entertainment business. Singing and being an entertainer might have been my dream when I was twelve, but I was able to create a new dream—a better dream more suited to me—from my original dream.

I do stand behind my lesson that you should never take "no" as an answer, but there are one or two exceptions to the rule. Some parents, educators, and specialists believe you should instill in children the belief that they can do anything they set out to do in life; that they can be "whatever their heart desires." I say, that's a nice notion but one that is not based in reality. The fact of the matter is, my parents didn't kill my dream by telling me to stop singing or bribing megarappers with Betty Crocker batter, but they also didn't unnecessarily lead me on and distract me from figuring out what I was really meant to do. Instead, they enabled me to explore the industry as a whole and find my place within it; a place that would appreciate and put to use my unique talents and vice versa. So while I took "no" as a final answer for my pop-star future, I redefined "no" and turned it on its head and found out that my musical instinct was actually right on—it was the execution that needed figuring out.

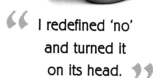

I redefined 'no' and turned it on its head.

When you try on a pair of new trendy heels, but they aren't the most comfortable fit, it doesn't necessarily mean the trend isn't for you.

Maybe it's the cut of the shoe, the width, or the arch. Don't abandon the trend, just try a different shoe. It's the same thing when you are reaching for a new goal. Just because the end result doesn't work out doesn't mean you are not on to something. My instinct was right all along about being involved in entertainment, but my compass just needed a shift. Can you look back on any of your "no" situations and find alternatives or see the possibilities for an avenue all your own *within* that situation? I bet if you look hard enough at your past "failed" attempts you'll realize they got you closer to where you are now. This is true whether it's your dating life, career ambitions, living situations, or educational pursuits.

Looking back, it seems I had many other encounters with the word *no*, and I remember seizing the opportunities to find a better way. Take summer camp, for example, where I met so many amazing people and actually two of my best friends, Juliet and Val, who are still friends today. For more than ten years my friends and I attended the same day camp. From the age of eight or nine years old we all planned to become counselors together when we reached the camp-approved age of fifteen. Being a counselor was a rite of passage into adulthood. What better measure of true responsibility than when a camp gives you authority over the welfare of younger children? The summer I turned fifteen was everything I anticipated it would be. There were four or five counselors per group of fifteen to twenty children. It was a blast, and I felt like our group of friendships grew stronger that summer and my love for the camp was sealed forever.

It was my summer home away from home. Besides sharing amazing memories with my camp friends, I was tasked with the normal duties of a camp counselor, which included watching over each girl in my group and escorting the children from activity to activity, whether it was swimming, basketball, archery, or even art class. We were not just babysitters for the girls; we were also people they could confide in; they looked up to us like big sisters. The activities were the same activities that I had participated in as a camper, but this time I was the one who the girls turned to.

> " The days of being on the bottom of the totem pole were behind me. I had paid my dues! "

When that summer came to an end I was sad to not be with my camp friends and the group of girls I watched over, but on the brighter side, I made more than $1,000 in tips and was excited for the next year when I would be sixteen and no longer a junior counselor. I'd be a full-fledged counselor and would be getting paid! The days of being on the bottom of the totem pole were behind me. I had paid my dues!

That winter we all waited for the camp to call us and invite us back as counselors again, but I was one longtime member who would not be coming back. The camp directors cited the reason as being my supposed inability to carry lunch and/or towels for my group. I could not believe this was happening to me. The previous summer we had all done equal amounts of work and no one ever said anything to me about not being able to carry the girls' lunches in a big linen bag (that looked like a laundry bag). I mean, *come on!* I had been going to the camp for ten years and now they just figured out that I could not do certain things? Did they think I would balance everything on my head?

I was devastated and cried for days. Who were they to tell me what I could and couldn't do? For ten years my parents had paid a lot of money for me to attend that camp, and all of sudden when I was eligible to finally get paid for the duties of a counselor I was no longer good enough? Why was this happening to me? I felt as if I had done something wrong and demanded the chance to speak with the camp directors to understand their decision. My mother called first and gave them a piece of her mind (to say the least), telling them to come up with a much better reason why I was not invited back; otherwise, she would call the newspapers, and worse, her lawyers, about this discrimination. (Seriously, don't mess with Mom.)

After the call I was still not satisfied. I've never been one to have my parents (or anyone else, for that matter) fight my battles, so I decided to call myself and possibly confront them in person. I called multiple times with the hopes that they would change their minds; however, no one would get on the phone with me. Finally, the son of the owner called me back. He tried to explain their decision, but I just could not comprehend their position: they weren't going to hire me back because I was physically unable to carry lunch or towels? I supposed they didn't want me for not being a good enough mule.

" I was always pushing myself to the limit to achieve anything I attempted. "

The owner's son was a man who had known me since I was five years old and always told me what a terrific inspiration I was to the other campers. On the phone I said to him, "How dare you treat me this way; I have been a loyal member of this camp for ten years and this is the way you treat me? You're the first person in my life to make me feel like I am incapable of doing something and making me feel handicapped, and I refuse to allow you or anyone at this camp to ever treat me like this again." I also told him that this was not last time he would hear from me!!

About fifteen minutes later the phone rang and on the other end was the camp representatives stating that they were sorry and never meant to make me feel this way, but they had a policy and could not go against it. They also said they had concerned parents who wondered what would happen if there were an emergency with one of their kids on my watch. I was baffled since this was the first time I had heard of such concerns and policies. The entire conversation was convoluted, which I suppose wasn't an accident.

It took me a long time to get over it because this was the first time I had felt handicapped, or better yet, incapable of doing something. I was always pushing myself to the limit to achieve anything I attempted. After about a week of feeling sorry for myself, my parents sat me down and said, "Lauren, you know what you are capable of and screw those idiots. You're a strong young woman, and sometimes people are ignorant, but you're the only one who can make yourself feel better, so get back on the horse and show everyone what you got!" That evening I called a few friends from camp to chat about what was going on, and they offered the same advice and vowed that if they went back, the camp would never be the same.

That next weekend I went to Ultissima (my parents' hair salon) and got a haircut, highlights, and a manicure, because on Monday I was going to begin interviewing for summer jobs. The camp directors were not going to defeat me! I proved that their decision could not get me down, and

I was hired by another local camp in the community as a counselor for kids under four years old, a job I kept for the next three summers.

Part of my "never take *no* for an answer" attitude comes from my parents' example. Clearly I learned how to stand up for myself by their actions toward doctors, parents, camp counselors, and others. And as you can see from their pep talks, they are not the enabling types. They fought on my behalf *against* special treatment and *for* the ability to enjoy things that other kids took pleasure in. I always assumed the world was my oyster. And why wouldn't it be? I was always up for a good time, never assumed I'd be treated differently because of my condition, and had big plans for my future. I guess my parents insulated me in a way from the idea that I was "special." And I am so grateful they did.

> " I always assumed the world was my oyster. "

By the time I got to college, I was emotionally prepared for the goals I set out to achieve. It was a pleasant time in my life. In fact, I loved Hofstra University. It was the first time I lived on my own. Dorm life gave me the kind of autonomy and independence any eighteen-year-old craves. I learned about myself and made great friends. The fact that I knew what I wanted to do for a career made classes easier for me than they are for so many other college students who go through four years of school and still enter the real world confused and uncertain about what they want to do.

The camaraderie and learning atmosphere of school were exhilarating, but getting real experience in the entertainment business became more important to me than getting straight As (or, in my case, Bs). Yes, I wanted to do well in school, but I also knew that academic achievement was only part of the equation if I wanted to get a good job in the very competitive world of show business. So I set about building on the internships I had started doing while still in high school. That kind of frontline experience is what employers are looking for (and makes the difference in their decision to hire you over someone who did not work during college).

I definitely wanted to be job-ready after graduation. I wasn't afraid of the hard work involved in simultaneously getting a degree and having an internship. Diligence and industriousness are in my blood. My dad always worked late—as I mentioned, my parents ran their own salon. There are few days off when you are a business owner, particularly when you work in one that is service-oriented. My two sisters (Addy and Emily) and I had to wait until 7:30 PM for him to come home so we could eat dinner as a family. We would always call the salon to ask if he had left for home because we were starving. Hey, when you're eight or ten years old, eating at 7:30 PM is like eating at midnight! Dad would tell us that his round-the-clock schedule was creating a better life for my sisters and me. "The more you work, the more you get," was a favorite phrase of his. Another, "Working pays for play," is one of his pearls of wisdom I live by today.

Getting a college internship at a radio station would be made easier by the fact that I was already an old hand at radio. My first apprenticeship started my senior year in high school at a local Long Island radio station, 92.7 WDRE FM. I had gone to a concert they sponsored (I'm a major music fan, as you've probably already guessed), and I was so excited about it that I called the promotions department and asked about interning. They could sense my enthusiasm and put me in the high-profile promotions department. Radio station promotion involves going to malls and concerts and handing out branded goods, like caps and mugs. I also helped the disc jockeys with their music lists, which I thought was an awesome responsibility.

> " They could sense my enthusiasm and put me in the high-profile promotions department. "

WDRE was my first taste of show biz and broadcasting, but I wanted to go bigger and better, and at the start of my sophomore year in college, I got an internship at Z100. It wasn't easy. I sent them my résumé literally every day. They recognized my tenacity and finally relented. That famous station was located in Secaucus, New Jersey. Hofstra was on Long Island. So I would drive from school to the station after classes, which took me more than an hour. Everyone thought I was crazy, but it was *so* worth it.

I spent two happy years at Z100, but I still wanted to expand my experience, so I set my sights on VH1. It's not easy to get an internship at the popular music video station today, and it was not back then either, as you can imagine. What college kid wouldn't want to work there? But I did get in, through sheer will and persistence (I used the same strategy that worked with Z100—I was relentless and consistent about sending my résumé to them and following up with phone calls). Plus, I had great experience from my radio days; they would be getting someone who could hit the ground running.

Even though I was still a full-time college student with a jam-packed class load, I worked at the music video station four days a week. I was learning a lot more at VH1 than I was at school, but there was no way I was going to leave college without a degree. I spent my time at VH1 in the talent-relations department in the station's fledgling Save the Music program, which provided music education for schools and my classes.

When my stint at the Save the Music program ended (the program still exists today), I went to PMK, the famous celebrity public relations firm, and asked if I could do two days a week there as an intern. They said yes, and I was immediately immersed in the world of celebrities.

> " I thought getting a paying job would be a piece of cake. "

Naturally, when I graduated I thought getting a paying job would be a piece of cake. After all, I knew so many people and had so much experience that I was certainly going to be the first on any company's list of contenders. It's true those internships got me in the door for an interview every time—I went on *thirty* of them. More often than not I'd be called back for second, sometimes even third, meetings. These conferences would go really well—the human-resource people and managers loved my experience. Wow! I'd have my pick of offers; how would I decide between them?

Nothing happened. No offers! I could not understand it. Then, an executive from one television company (who will remain nameless) said to me, "I love you, and I really want to hire you, but I have to ask if you need special health insurance? You're handicapped and my boss wants to know if you need to be treated differently." That opened up my eyes as to why I wasn't getting job offers, despite the fact that I was a good fit at every company I met with. It never occurred to me that my condition would stop anyone from hiring me, especially since I had never asked for or expected any kind of special consideration because of it. That was the last thing I wanted, in fact.

At that point finding a job had nothing to do with money—I would have taken any salary. I just wanted to start working. "No" was simply not an option for me. If it took sixty interviews, or one hundred, I would just keep plugging away. My thirty-first interview was with Markham/Novell Communications, a celebrity public relations firm that represented people like Jim Henson and nonpeople like the Muppets. Before I even had an interview, I was told to fax a handwritten letter to Arthur Novell, the main partner in the firm, explaining why I wanted to work for him.

Arthur believed in handwriting analysis, and apparently mine pleased him. He hired me as soon as I walked in the door—at a whopping $21,000 a year I commuted from Long Island to Manhattan everyday, and while I loved the work, the travel really became a hassle. I wanted to move into the city and have the ultimate urban lifestyle. My parents were understandably nervous, but commuting by train was cramping my style. I found a place called Tracy Towers on 24th Street and 2nd Avenue. Two of my best friends were close by: Samantha, who lived across the street from the high-rise, and Jason, who lived on Lexington and 23rd Street. This reassured my family that I'd have a Manhattan support system should I need one. So I settled in and worked for Markham/Novell and loved every minute of it (you'll hear more about those crazy times in the next chapter).

Getting a job was not my first personal experience of dealing with "no" and getting to "yes." But it *was* the first time that accepting "no" as an answer would have had dire consequences for my future. I wanted to work in the entertainment field, and if I had not gone on one more interview, I might have been defeated by those who thought I would need "special treatment or assistance." Today, everyone around me knows not to say "no" to me or to accept it as an answer from anyone else unless there is excellent reasoning behind it. I teach my staff that the word "no" does not lead to growth. If someone tells you "no", you have to back right up to them with "why not?" and expect a good—and justified— answer. I believe anything can be done, and

> " I teach my staff that the word 'no' does not lead to growth. "

"no" is often simply the lazy way out. It's the shortest way to avoid going the extra mile, and it doesn't impress or stop me.

For instance, I am not afraid to call anyone: presidents of networks, the mayor of New York City, heads of state, it doesn't matter. "No" is not an option if I am to be successful at my job. I use a variety of techniques when I'm confronted with a skeptical or resistant colleague. Mostly it's all in how you speak to someone. I'll say, "I understand your point, so why don't we try it this way?" and then present another way to accomplish my task. I just keep going back until I get what I want, and I make sure that the other people feel they are making an important contribution. The trick is to stick to your guns without being arrogant and without making other people feel less important or bossed around. In your effort to challenge naysayers, do it respectfully, so everyone is happy, feels important, and is doing something he or she is proud of. Most important, keep your ears open.

It might be necessary for a "no" to come at you, but always be ready to convert "no" into the workable alternatives that will lead you to "yes." My "tendency toward tenacity" has paid off every time. Don't be deterred on your own rocky road—even if one road on your journey does not work out (in my case it was singing), because another one will present itself. And those roads might be tough to go down, but that's no excuse for sitting things out on the curb.

When it comes to naysayers, please keep in mind the following:

1. **"No" is rarely as final as it sounds.** Find out why you're getting the objection, and deal with the root of the issue. Listen to the concerns and take them into consideration when revisiting your idea/suggestion/question. Your intent should be to design an alternative and gain the respect and attention of people who realize you don't work in a bubble, and take their reactions into serious consideration. It may take a few times, but you'll be surprised about how much closer to "yes" you will get every time.

" Your intent should be to design an alternative and gain the respect and attention of people who realize you don't work in a bubble. "

2. **If the "no" is stubborn (in my case, becoming a pop star), find an equally suitable alternative as soon as you can.** Never let the "no" get you stuck in a place you don't want to be. Get going, even if it takes thirty-one times, or one hundred times. If you really want something, a "no" or two or isn't going to stop you, is it?

3. **People sometimes say "no" because they**

are worried, afraid, tired, or too busy to deal; give them some time and go back in with information they will need to see that their worries, fears, exhaustion, and schedule have nothing to do with you or what you are asking for. Timing, after all, is everything.

4. **Be nice.** "No" is generally melted in a surprisingly easy manner when confronted with charm and understanding. And if that doesn't work, the fact that you were nice about it will help you get the "yes" you want the next time around. Graciousness will take you far.

5. **Never say "no" to yourself—you are the one person you can depend on to always say "yes"!** You know the old saying: *Get out of your own way.* I would have been so justified, after thirty job interviews, to just forget it and change career ambitions to something a bit safer and easier, but if I turned my back on myself, what use would I be to anyone else anywhere else I went?

6. **More often than not, naysayers are also non-doers, paralyzed by their own fears and hoping to keep you stuck too;** so when hearing "no," again consider the source. It will be easy to move on after that.

CHAPTER

4

PAY YOUR DUES

LAUREN'S LESSON:
REJECTION CAN BE YOUR
GREATEST ALLY AND LEAD
TO YOUR DREAMS

One bachelor of arts degree in communications from Hofstra University, five amazing internships, and thirty-one interviews later, I *finally* landed a job in public relations at Markham/Novell, a celebrity public relations firm. One of the owners, Arthur Novell, was a tough boss—very old school, with many old-fashioned idiosyncrasies—but he was a wonderful teacher. He ran his office like a talent agency from a 1950s movie—with lots of phones ringing, established clients given the red-carpet treatment, and potential clients vying for attention. He would fight with his partner all the time, so there was a lot of bickering and door slamming, but overall their unique dynamic led to success. And then there was his passion for handwriting analysis.

Before I get more into the details of my first job, let's go back to the thirty-one interviews I went on before I landed my first job. Without walking you through the arduous process of being rejected over and over, I'm afraid the momentous event of my actually landing a full-time, paying job will be anticlimactic. Plus, I've run into some of the people who uttered the "thanks but no thanks" response since I started my career, and they are actually astonished by my current success in the business world. It's always satisfying to say to these folks, "thank you for not hiring me," like you would say to an ex-boyfriend, "thanks for breaking up with me," while you are holding the hand of your hot new beau. A little F.U. never hurt anyone (at least the ones who have ever said it!). Fresh out of college with five amazing internships under my belt plus recommendations money couldn't buy, my confidence was peaked, and I thought I would land a job within days of graduating. I began sending out my résumé about two to three months before I graduated. Almost every time I sent it, I got a callback, and if I didn't, I would follow up with them until they called me back. I was lining up interviews left and right. It

> It was only a matter of time before I landed my dream job and was going to move to NYC and be an independent and fabulous woman.

was only a matter of time before I landed my dream job and was going to move to NYC and be an independent and fabulous woman. Well, as you already know, it wasn't exactly that easy. Like I said before, it took me thirty-one interviews to land a job, and by the end I was ready to throw in the towel and go back to school to be a teacher like my mother wanted me to be. My strong perception of how the job-scoring process would go was shattered. I was interviewed by almost every single hot PR company, television network, and radio station in the metropolitan area. First I would have a phone interview with the human resources manager, which led to an invitation for a face-to-face meeting with the hiring manager. The phone interviews always went well. I am good on the phone: articulate, concise, approachable, passionate, and enthusiastic, so these usually led to the in-person interview. Then I would walk in and meet them, and you could tell by the dropped jaws that they were nothing short of shocked and certainly thrown for a loop. Perhaps I should have included my photo on my résumé or mentioned my physique to them so they weren't caught off guard. In all fairness, how could they have been prepared otherwise? But, while the thought of doing this did infiltrate this brain of mine, I admit I was afraid that I wouldn't get an initial call before I even had the opportunity to wow them with my natural zest for life and ability to communicate my intellect. So, I was damned if I did, and damned if I didn't. Aside from unemployed and broke, that is the crappiest place to be. If I only could have been like Edward Cullen from *Twilight* and read minds, I would've known right off the bat that my stature freaked them out and they were never going to hire me. They loved my experience and personality, but when push came to shove, I was beat out by another candidate who had less experience than I did. Can I say that it was 100 percent because of my handicap? No, but why time after time they would go with someone else is beyond me.

❝ I was damned if I did, and damned if I didn't. ❞

One time, when I was on my second interview with a company and it was going really well, I was asked, "Do you have any other questions about insurance, because I am not sure if you need special insurance." I was just dumbfounded. It all became clear right then why I was not being hired. I went back to my parents' house that night filled with anger and just cried. I felt defeated by my handicap for the second time in my life; the first time since the summer camp did not rehire me. Did hiring managers think I was not as creative or educated as other candidates because I walk with crutches? Could they not see all my experience and references?

Finally, a very serious prospect called back, and this time all they asked me to do was write a handwritten letter about why I wanted to work at Markham/Novell. Within forty-eight hours of mailing my letter, I received a phone call informing me that president and owner Arthur Novell wanted to meet me. I went in and he hired me on the spot. It might not have been at either the celebrity public relations and/or the MTV job that I truly wanted, but it was an amazing experience and a job I will never forget. In this business you get beat down a million times, but there are also a million rewards for a job done well, and that is what I was determined to do. The other jobs I interviewed for couldn't have given me the opportunity to grow and learn like Markham/Novell did. So in the end, I was where I needed to be, gaining experience that I would need for my next endeavor, whatever that would be.

Arthur was so particular in the way things had to be done, in nutty kinds of ways. I took it all in stride—that's show biz. For instance, all of his telephone messages had to be printed out on green paper in an Excel format. If he couldn't return the calls that day, I would have to write them out again, this time on pink paper, for the next day. So his desk was inevitably covered in paper graphs in a preppy color combo. His filing system was also very obscure, and he was extremely finicky about the way files were labeled and organized. Today, I believe many young people fresh out of college would not stand for this, as technology has changed the way we handle administrative duties; however, I was not about to give up on the dream I had because my boss wanted things done in a certain way. Who was I to tell him I thought it should be done a different way? He was already in his late fifties and had a very successful public relations business.

A lot of people would have walked away from that job—that would have been too bad. If I had left in disgust or out of exasperation, I would have missed out on so much. Arthur was quirky, but I learned a lot from him, and I appreciated the fact that he saw tons of potential in me. Arthur let me grow. He taught me how to be political, when to speak and when to stay silent; when to show my ideas and when to keep them close to the vest. I learned about respect from him. For example, he had so much regard for the Henson family.

> " I learned so many things on the job that you just don't learn in a classroom. "

Jim had passed away a year before I started, so we began dealing directly with his widow, Jane. We all called her Mrs. Henson, and I only spoke to her when she asked me a question. Arthur made me understand that because I was new to the business I had to wait my turn a bit and not make

READER/CUSTOMER CARE SURVEY

We care about your opinions! Please take a moment to fill out our online Reader Survey at **http://survey.hcibooks.com.**
As a **"THANK YOU"** you will receive a **VALUABLE INSTANT COUPON** towards future book purchases
as well as a **SPECIAL GIFT** available only online! Or, you may mail this card back to us.

(PLEASE PRINT IN ALL CAPS)

First Name _____ MI. _____ Last Name _____

Address _____ City _____

State _____ Zip _____ Email _____

1. Gender
- ❑ Female   ❑ Male

2. Age
- ❑ 8 or younger
- ❑ 9-12   ❑ 13-16
- ❑ 17-20   ❑ 21-30
- ❑ 31+

3. Did you receive this book as a gift?
- ❑ Yes   ❑ No

4. Annual Household Income
- ❑ under $25,000
- ❑ $25,000 - $34,999
- ❑ $35,000 - $49,999
- ❑ $50,000 - $74,999
- ❑ over $75,000

5. What are the ages of the children living in your house?
- ❑ 0 - 14   ❑ 15+

6. Marital Status
- ❑ Single
- ❑ Married
- ❑ Divorced
- ❑ Widowed

7. How did you find out about the book?
(please choose one)
- ❑ Recommendation
- ❑ Store Display
- ❑ Online
- ❑ Catalog/Mailing
- ❑ Interview/Review

8. Where do you usually buy books?
(please choose one)
- ❑ Bookstore
- ❑ Online
- ❑ Book Club/Mail Order
- ❑ Price Club (Sam's Club, Costco's, etc.)
- ❑ Retail Store (Target, Wal-Mart, etc.)

9. What subject do you enjoy reading about the most?
(please choose one)
- ❑ Parenting/Family
- ❑ Relationships
- ❑ Recovery/Addictions
- ❑ Health/Nutrition
- ❑ Christianity
- ❑ Spirituality/Inspiration
- ❑ Business Self-help
- ❑ Women's Issues
- ❑ Sports

10. What attracts you most to a book?
(please choose one)
- ❑ Title
- ❑ Cover Design
- ❑ Author
- ❑ Content

TAPE IN MIDDLE; DO NOT STAPLE

BUSINESS REPLY MAIL

FIRST-CLASS MAIL PERMIT NO 45 DEERFIELD BEACH, FL

POSTAGE WILL BE PAID BY ADDRESSEE

Health Communications, Inc.
3201 SW 15th Street
Deerfield Beach FL 33442-9875

FOLD HERE

Comments

assumptions about relationships or take liberties I had not yet earned. I speak to a lot of people who won't or can't put their egos aside, bite the bullet, and pay their dues. You can't just walk into a company and expect to run the place. In my domain, it's the closest thing to an apprenticeship, and apprentices work hard, know their place, and are rewarded later on *big-time*.

I learned so many things on the job that you just don't learn in a classroom. For example, Arthur taught me how to write an effective press release. Jeanine, the PR supervisor who oversaw everything in the office, was my savior. She taught me how to become better organized, and more important, she helped me learn how to disseminate my ideas in a concise manner for others to understand my way of thinking. She, like Arthur, saw my creative potential and passion for success, so on occasion she took me along on pitch meetings to producers at Fox or the *Today Show* and allowed me to interject my creative thoughts into the meeting. She, too, helped me with writing press releases. Overall, she was an ally, a confidant and someone I respected tremendously.

Arthur brought me to important meetings with clients, and would sit me down and go over the agenda with me. He listened to my ideas and strategized them, planning how and when to present them in the meeting to achieve the most impact. He protected me from my own ideas too, as many times I needed to hone my understanding of the impact they would or would not have on the business. For example, when Miss Piggy launched her first perfume, Moi, I immediately wanted to create street teams to have people dress up like Miss Piggy and give away samples of the perfume. Arthur loved the idea but said there was only one Miss Piggy, and the Henson family might think that we were mocking the brand. I had a lot of spunk and enthusiasm (still do), and he did not want me to look like an idiot and come across as overzealous to the Henson executives and family. Therefore we decided to plan out our thoughts before we approached anyone with my ideas. Sometimes when a good idea arises, I feel like a kid in a candy store, but today before I present any idea I sit down and ask myself, *How can we execute this, and what's in it for the brand and the consumer?*

Then there were lessons on taking control of the room and commanding the right kind of attention—all tactics I use today in the entertainment business. Twelve years later I still love commanding a room's attention. Attitude—the right one—can help you take command of a room, a job, or your life. Last week we had a

> **Sometimes when a good idea arises, I feel like a kid in a candy store.**

seminar and the senior vice president was trying to get the seventy people who had gathered in the auditorium to settle down. I could hear her trying to get everyone's attention, so I went over to her and said, "You have to be louder." She was skeptical and a bit timid, so I offered to take care of it. No microphone needed with my voice (maybe those singing lessons did me some good after all—I know how to project). I announced to the room, "Can everyone turn around and take a seat? We are trying to begin this seminar and we'd appreciate your attention." Well, wouldn't you know it, they all sat down.

Taking command of a room comes easy to me, but a lot of that is due to what I learned from Arthur. Other tips I learned from him:

- Never step on other people's words. Let someone speak their mind before you interrupt.
- Never interject until the person has finished speaking (this is a hard one for me since I have a tendency, in my enthusiasm, to speak over people).
- If there is someone in the room who outranks you, and you think his or her idea needs work, never say so. Instead, say something like, "I do agree with you on this point, but what if we thought of this other point in a different way?" The point is to enhance people, not ridicule them. Besides, I do buy into that adage that there is no such thing as a stupid

idea. Ideas lead to other ideas, and if you don't impede them, they ultimately lead to the BIG IDEA.

* Always build up your boss; if you build him or her up, he or she will build you up. You have to make people above you feel that way. If you make them feel they are beneath you, you are going to get nowhere fast.

I worked for Arthur for a year and half—it was like getting a master's degree in public relations, as I learned more in this time frame than I did in four years of college. After about nine months on the job I was getting restless and wanted to have more experience—and money. Twenty-one thousand dollars did not go very far in New York. Arthur gave me a raise of $2,500 a year (gee whiz, after taxes that came to about twenty-two dollars a week, which was the same amount as a subway pass!) and told me that if I brought in a client, I would get a percentage of the client's monthly retainer. (That's another lesson I learned from Arthur: incentives are impor-

> ❝ Always build up your boss; if you build him or her up, he or she will build you up. ❞

tant.) So bring in a client I did—a good one: Advanced Research Press/Twin Labs, which at the time was the largest vitamin company in the country. The company was about to relaunch their first magazine titled *Muscular Development.* I had a friend who knew one of the owners and asked them to introduce me. I called on Steve Blechman, who was in charge of marketing and product development, and pitched him my ideas on bringing in a PR agency to help them relaunch their magazine. After I brought in the client, I worked day in and day out research-ing different media outlets to get them press. Health was not my strong suit but that did not stop me from getting the job done and securing twenty interviews in four months. I was just twenty-three years old. *Not bad*, I thought! And the client liked me so much that they made me the offer I could not refuse: director of communications at more than twice the salary I was making with Novell. Their offices were on Long Island, so I had a reverse commute from the city.

Arthur was upset, but he knew where I was heading and he gave me his blessings. I think I was more upset about leaving than he was, because I liked my job even though we did not see eye to eye on everything. Looking back on it, Arthur helped mold me into the tough businesswoman I am today. I owe him and the people I worked with a huge thank-you for allowing me to creatively execute my ideas. I was at Twin Labs for six months and realized it was a mis-take. I did not like the reverse commute, and I felt as if I was not with my peers. Everyone seemed to be older than I was and married with kids—not great for a single girl on the go. More important, I was not learning anything new. I needed to get back to my life in the city, so I quietly started to look for another job.

This time, I didn't have to go on thirty-one interviews to find something better. I knew people who knew people (so handy!) and heard that *TV Guide* magazine was hiring. I went straight to the guy who was in charge of finding the right person and got my foot (high heel and all) in the door. He knew who I was and introduced me to the right people: by the time I was twenty-four I had created a well-respected reputation in the PR field. The company was starting a division called the Web Guide, which was part of a broad Internet strategy. I was charged with building up this new business, which I did. And over six years I built myself up too, working my way up from manager to a director. My creative juices were always flowing, and eventually I was able to create my own position with the help of the amazing management who believed in my

> My career truly soared, and I was living the business life I'd always dreamed of.

craft. My career truly soared, and I was living the business life I'd always dreamed of. I would travel between New York City and Los Angeles at least six or seven times a year and began to establish a Los Angeles base of contacts in the television arena, which helped to take my career to the next level. By the time I was ready to leave *TV Guide,* I had the entertainment community in my pocket.

After my tenure at *TV Guide,* Hearst Magazines hired me because they knew the kind of work I did. They allowed me to sculpt the position I created at *TVG* and format into my current position, one that had never existed at the company before I came along. There is more to the story of my career trajectory, but the point I want to make here is that you should always give people and opportunities a chance, even if they seem intimidating, a bit odd, or challenging—like Arthur—and even if they ultimately don't work out, like Advanced Research Press/Twin Labs.

Without taking these chances, I wouldn't have been able to network and therefore have the inside track on job openings and other opportunities. Without the thirty-one rejected interviews, I wouldn't have gauged just how much I wanted to be in PR and marketing. If you stay the course despite thirty-one doors being shut on you, the right people will start noticing your endurance and passion instead of your shortcomings, and in my case, that was my interview turning point.

One of the things I love most about my job experience, as

faulty as some of it has been, is that I have been surrounded by eccentrics, oddballs, and even outright jerks. You also need to know how to determine those oddballs and eccentrics that are worth sticking with and those that aren't. Meeting the eccentrics exposed me to so much more of the world's depth. Instead of the homogenous upbringing I had on Long Island, I learned people existed out there with hobbies and interests that I'd never even heard of. Oddballs and eccentrics can be the most creative people, and they can inspire your own creativity tenfold. They can also help draw out the inner oddball in you, to help you break away from your safe place and try out new out-of-the-box ideas and perspectives. Basically, in work and in life, the more different types of people you are exposed to, the more you grow and the better you'll be for it. That's the key to job experience: it's about the people as much as the details of the task.

> " It's about the people as much as the details of the task. "

Then there are the complete assholes . . . the ones who are offensive and ignorant and who are just a plain, sad fact of life that you can do nothing about. For instance, there is a guy I worked with who would randomly tell me "short and hand-icapped" jokes. If we were riding in the elevator together, he'd just spontaneously come up with some really stupid one-liner. Finally I said to him, "Joe, you are being *quite* politically incorrect," and his response was that he could talk to me that way because his kid had a disability as well. Huh? Some people have no filter. Most of the time I don't let people like this affect me, and you shouldn't either, because it's not worth the trouble and effort. We've all got more important stuff on our plates than to be distracted by these kinds of head cases. (Because this is such an important topic, I actually dedicated Chapter 5 to addressing these toxic types.)

But there are times when you do have to straighten people out. I have come in contact with people who look at me or look at my crutches and assume I don't have a brain or can't do certain things. I know my limitations, so I don't need other people to do it for me, especially when they have no idea who I am and what I can do. No one should ever be allowed to set limits for you.

That's why I wanted to write a chapter about paying your dues. When you don't, you are engaging in a self-limiting behavior. What seems like nonsensical jumping through hoops will actually teach you the most about whatever it is you are after. Picking up knowledge can be accomplished everywhere you go, if you just have the right attitude and use every opportunity (as shitty as you think it may be at the time) to learn something, meet someone, try something new, or make a networking connection. When you turn down positions or opportunities that seem "beneath" you, you can gyp yourself in a major way.

Especially in these competitive times, you have to take what you can get and then make it what you need it to be. Quit looking at everything or every job as a dead end, even if it's not your "dream." You'll get there. It took me a lot of time to prove myself, and when I did, I still needed to learn what kind of job and environment suited

> " Let rejection teach you, and the lessons you learn from each failed attempt will lead the way to where you are supposed to be. "

me—and I'm still learning, which is the best part of building a career! Learning. The minute you stop learning, you stop growing. And stunting yourself is just not cool.

If you are on your way to making the *Guinness Book of World Records* for the most rejected interviews, always remember my thirty-one interviews. I am literally like the Baskin-Robbins of failed job attempts. But the sweet life is ahead if you just keep at it the same way I did. Hey, even ice cream isn't made without churning, and churn is what you will need to do to make your dreams come true. Let rejection teach you, and the lessons you learn from each failed attempt will lead the way to where you are supposed to be. I can confidently say that the accumulation of all my rejected moments (career or otherwise) led me to the writing of this book, so where will you let it take you?

When dealing with rejections, turn to clichés. They are true for a reason and really make the most sense: "When one door closes, somebody opens a window." "If at first you don't succeed, try, try again." "Never give up." Okay, okay. I say this tongue-in-cheek. I know these phrases can make you scream, especially when you're down-and-out. So if you've been kicked when you're down a few too many times, here are a few things I suggest you keep in mind:

- All it takes is one "yes" to change the course of your life.
- Confidence, perseverance, and determination are the keys to success.
- Just because someone cannot see the obvious talents you possess doesn't mean they're not there.

Like Dr. Seuss says, "Laugh often, dream big, reach for the stars!"

5

FOES, FRENEMIES, F'EM

LAUREN'S LESSON:
TAKE INVENTORY OF THE COMPANY YOU KEEP AND CLEAN HOUSE EVERY ONCE IN A WHILE

We've all heard the maxim "There are two certainties in life: death and taxes," but I believe there is a third: dealing with toxic people. In many cases, there's also a fourth: coexisting with *stupid* people. The issue is that these toxic, or stupid, or sometimes the dangerous combination of toxically stupid people can really get under your skin and ruin your day, your mood, and sometimes more, *if* you let them. The trick is to overcome this before you have to take a Xanax to calm your nerves, which is much easier said than done! In this electronic age of Facebook friends, you can run into other "f" words like foes and faux pas that you can get caught up in and be distracted by. Then there are text wars and . . . oh . . . it's all just digital drama! E-mail doesn't help either. With so many professionals choosing to communicate mainly via the Internet, misunderstandings in context can happen; sometimes people are just plain ballsier in e-mails and instant messages and will insult you or be condescending. We all have run into a colleague or friend who in person is as sweet as sugar, but is outright rude in e-mail.

Then you have the "special" people, the type I am lucky enough to run across on the streets of Manhattan (or really any city I am in) on a daily basis. Being who I am, or looking the way I do (God forbid!), I get the doozies coming out of the woodwork to injure my pride, insult my intelligence, and just plain treat me like the freak show they think I am. (I think it's my cross to bear—to be a moron- or idiot-magnet.) The stares alone could put you into a deep depression. The one that bothers me the most is the continuous stare that resembles rubbernecking—when someone passes me as I walk across the street and turns his head to watch me while he continues walking in the opposite direction. I can understand it sometimes; I mean, how many four-feet-two-inch women are there in the world who wear four-inch heels and crutch around Manhattan like they own it? To say I have had to build a thick

> " To say I have had to build a thick skin is an understatement. "

skin is an understatement. It's more like armor. But it has taken me time to figure out that people are people. Some are friends, some are foes, and some are the worst kind: frenemies—the ones who, on the surface, act like your friends and then stab you in the back at some point.

I would bank on the fact that you, too, are dealing with stupid, snide, toxic people—at home, at work, at school, at play, even in line at the ladies' room. And I would also bet there are times when you are paying just a little too much attention to the negative crap—the blatant attempts to scorn you and make you feel like a lowlife. The time you spend lamenting over the negativity is precious, my friend, and you just gave that time away—gave your power over to STUPID PEOPLE. I am guilty as charged of doing the same, but I came to a point where I just didn't want to deal with it anymore, and I want to offer you some help to stop buying into the soulless acts of which you may be a victim.

My attitude can be summed up in three words: Let It Roll. I've made a habit of letting a lot of stupid things go that might get to other people, the kinds of ridiculous stuff that other people throw at me because clearly they are bored with their own lives.

For instance, I was in St. Lucia with my sister Emily and friend Brigette for my thirty-first birthday. We were walking down one of the main streets in town on our way to get dinner, and a homeless man who was walking with a limp came up to us and rather aggressively singled me out. He literally walked in front of me, stood there, and said, "Hey you, the little girl, I know how you feel." I just smiled, said "thank you," and kept walking. Well, another person might have taken offense, or been upset or scared, and let an exchange like that ruin their day. But this was a stranger, and I was on a beautiful island vacation (which last time I checked was not an all-expenses-paid excursion), so I was not about to waste my time being preoccupied with how a strange, rude man on the street could make me feel bad. No way—I had a tan to work on!

There are many other stories I could tell, but my two favorites have to do with dogs. One time I was having drinks with my Hearst colleagues at the SoHo Grand Hotel, located on trendy West Broadway, on their beautiful outside terrace in New York City, and I excused myself to go to the bathroom. I climbed about thirty steps (I know, because I counted them . . .) of an outside staircase and then walked into this beautifully lighted bathroom that boasted an amazing Venetian mirror as its centerpiece. I was in line behind two people. As I waited, a woman came

> " I could not believe my ears! Did this woman just compare me to an *umbrella*? "

out of the stall with a small dog tucked under her arm, the pose made famous by Paris Hilton. My first thought was, *A dog in the bathroom? Who was using the stall? The dog or the lady?* (Hey, it's New York City and weirder things have happened in bathroom stalls.) Anyway, I made my way to a stall, which was only about four steps, and the little dog started barking at me. The dog's owner, a petite woman wearing yoga clothes, apologized and then said to me, "I am sorry, but my dog has never seen anyone like you before. He is also afraid of umbrellas." I could not believe my ears! Did this woman just compare me to an *umbrella?* Was she insane? I retorted, "Okay . . . well, I have never been compared to an umbrella, but I am just here to go to the bathroom in peace."

I was kind of furious, but at the same time I could not stop laughing; perhaps my laughter was a mechanism to prevent me from crying. I went back and told my colleagues about the woman's comment, and all I could do was laugh. Everyone at the table was astonished; one of my colleagues, Jennifer, was so irate that someone would actually speak to me in that manner that she wanted to go and find the woman. Finally the woman walked out of the bathroom, and I pointed her out to Jennifer, who just couldn't help herself. She walked directly over to the woman and said, "You know, ma'am, you're a special kind of stupid, and you should not be in the business of comparing people to anything, especially umbrellas. Maybe your dog belongs at home and is just nervous to be at a lounge, and is not afraid of my friend at all."

Anyway, I took it in stride. The woman apologized to me and then I went back to my dirty vodka martini, which I very much needed by that time.

What is it with rude people, especially rude people with dogs? Now don't get me wrong, I absolutely love dogs and hope to have a little black-and-white puppy one day, despite my other run-in with a woman and her dog. Here's what happened.

> " Her dog had mistaken my crutch for a hydrant or some other toilet! "

I was on my way to work at *TV Guide* and I got off the F train at Rockefeller Center, walked up the steps to 6th Avenue, and was standing on the corner of 48th Street waiting for the light to turn green so I could walk across the street, when a dog peed on my crutch. I almost freaked out, but I tried not to take it out on the dog. I gently pushed the dog and starting yelling at his owner. "Oh my God, your dog is peeing on my crutch, please stop him right now!" The woman looked at me in amazement and snapped, "How dare you try and move my dog." Was this woman serious? Her dog had mistaken my crutch for a hydrant or some other toilet!

"You're a special kind of stupid" has to be one of the best statements I have ever heard, and it really sums up the way some people react to anyone who is different. Didn't your mother ever tell you, "If you have nothing nice to say, don't say it at all"?

Obsessing about slights or threats, coworkers, boyfriends, and on and on can become a full-time job, and you never get anything else done. Why waste time on playing the same record over and over again in your head? It is so simple to forget about the daily exchanges that are of no help to you and move forward with what you want to do.

Okay, so that covers the people we meet on the street and over whom we have no control, but what about the people with whom we actually surround ourselves? When we are young we tend to roll with crowds with whom we don't have things in common or who are beneath us in some way, but we can justify this choice with the need to have a social life, to have fun, or even to gain popularity. But have you noticed that as you get older, your tolerance for people's actions or your willingness to hang with people who you know are toxic or don't reciprocate your friendship is waning? That diminished capacity to spend your valuable time with screwballs is a good thing! Maybe it's because as we get older we have less spare time, and as anyone who stayed awake in economics class can tell you, the less spare time, the more valuable it becomes. So it's really no wonder that we'd rather sit at home alone and watch *The Real House-wives of New Jersey* than sit around a hot, crowded club talking with people with whom we have nothing in common. It's time to maximize this newfound maturity and translate it into weaning out the wieners and being particular about our select group of friends. When we get older we become more discerning naturally, and we need to hone our skills now that we are using our time and energy to actively choose who we allow "in." Where to begin?

Expect the best from people right from the get-go. Let's use my attitude toward medical care as an odd (but apropos) example. It's very simple: I will only go to the best. I do not like to go on other people's references (except those of other doctors or of my physical therapist, Carolyn), even though word of mouth from friends is a common means of finding a health-care provider. I have to research a doctor or institution myself, and when I go in I say, "I am here because you are a specialist, so prove it." I know more about my situation than most doctors know, so I never waste time treating a doctor as if he or she is a

> " You really don't know who your friends are until you start facing challenges. "

god or has special knowledge. The doctor should be my partner, and I can't waste time with someone who doesn't know what he or she is talking about.

In business, it's the same approach. I tell people, "I am coming to you because I hear you are great and I expect you to know what you're doing." Most projects can be completed very quickly if you want to do them, and they'll never get done if you don't. Therefore, I always try to discern the attitude that people have about the task at hand. I know after five minutes if I want someone on my team or not. That notion goes for friends too. I know if we will get along and understand each other. I look at people's body language, access their attitudes, and listen to their speech. Are they looking me in the eye? Are they enthusiastic? Can they articulate their ideas well? Are they trying to bullshit me?

So, if I expect my doctors to be my partners and my team members to be genuine, why wouldn't I put the same expectations on those in my social circle? They say that as you get older, you'll start losing friends. They also say that you really don't know who your friends are until you start facing challenges. I guess both are intertwined, since as we get older, we tend to encounter more complex situations; today I do have fewer friends than I did back in high school, but friendship is extremely important to me, and most of my very good friends have been in my life since I was a child. I'd rather have a life raft of four or five and stay afloat than a boatload and sink!

I admit that sustaining genuine friendships for

twenty-five to thirty years without falling out of touch or growing apart is a rarity, but to me, my friendships are part of my daily routine. For instance, I met Juliet, Jason, Jill, Val, and Samantha all before I was a teenager, and today we still speak at least a few times a month. We all now live in different places and countries but somehow our friendships are still strong.

Even though I have been able to sustain such amazing friendships throughout my life, I have also met people over the years (especially in my twenties) who have been eliminated as quickly as they came in because they were mean and deceitful. I was traveling back and forth to Los Angeles for some time and met some amazing people; however, I also met a man who almost tore down everything I'd built up in my life.

❝ I was just taken by him, and the relationship was blossoming. ❞

I remember it vividly . . . I was having cocktails with my colleague Allison (from *TV Guide*) at the Beverly Hills Hotel, which is one of the most famous hotels in Los Angeles because many celebrities rent or own bungalows there. A man who had a presence like no other man I'd ever met came over to speak with me, and he truly took my breath away with his stature and how he described himself. We spoke for hours, and at the end of the night we exchanged phone numbers. I was so excited because a man had never spoken to me before in such a manner and taken such interest in who I was or what I wanted. Allison was also charmed by him. The next day he called, and he took me to dinner at the ultratrendy Asian restaurant, Mr. Chow in Beverly Hills. Over the next week I spent all my free time with him, and I even met his family. I was just taken by him, and the relationship was blossoming.

For the next few months we spoke daily and he would either come to New York or I'd be in Los Angeles, so we never went a month without seeing each other. However, during my third trip back to Los Angeles after meeting him he began to show his true colors. All of sudden, he said he'd run out of money, lost his house, and needed to stay with me at my hotel. This was a behavior that I had never seen before in anyone I had ever met. How could he not have a house or an apartment but drive a Rolls-Royce worth almost $300,000? He began treating me like a second-class citizen and just wanted me to pay for everything. I started questioning him a lot. No matter what I asked him, he would turn on the charm and change the topic. He would tell me that everything was okay and not to worry; that we were together and that was all that mattered. I believed him and gave him whatever he needed. This went on for weeks, and I started to get angry because all he wanted from me was to get into the right places and parties, and he would freely spend my hard-earned money.

Finally, the relationship ended in a horrible way, leaving me with a huge amount of debt that took me more than three years to repay, but luckily I have never heard from him again. I learned so many lessons throughout this relationship: The number one lesson was not to trust people unless they have first proven themselves to be trustworthy. Compliments are just words that can form a well-thought-out sentence, but actions speak louder than words. I now apply this lesson to everyone new who I meet. Sometimes you get distracted, but in the end your core values always come back.

> ❝ Expect the best from those who will fill your inner circle. ❞

But the friendship and relationship things are a two-way street, and just as in business, I will never tell a friend I can do something or offer him or her something (my time, my attention, whatever), when I know I can't deliver. If people know who they are getting up front, as a friend, colleague, and/or boss, relationships will thrive. There are no surprises, false pretenses, or resentments later on. You can't disappoint people if you come at them with who you really are from the get-go. But to make an impression, so many of us try to be the best versions of ourselves, and that gets exhausting. (Even I sometimes find myself overcompensating or offering too much of my time and energy toward a friendship or relationship, and that's a recipe for burnout.) Once the ruse is up (and there always comes a time), the friendship is over.

I expect the same from the people around me, personally, professionally, and medically. And I try to be around people who are either already great or have the potential to be great. Surrounding yourself with people *like you* will make life easier.

So go ahead and be picky! Expect the best from those who will fill your inner circle. Determine who is as much of a friend to you as you are to them. Who do you actually want to spend your precious time with, and does he or she bring out the very best in you? This is the best part of adult relationships: getting rid of those who tire you out, breaking up with bitches who are way too high-maintenance for you, and just taking control of your cadre. It means you really have gotten to know who you are and are defining yourself further by the company you keep. And you can tell a lot about a person by the company she keeps.

When dealing with the Fs in your life, remember:

1. **Take it as a compliment:** If you are insulted by a stranger (or anyone else, for that matter); remember that they considered you for enough time to actually form the insult. That's much more time than you'd ever spend on them!

2. **Laugh:** Calling myself a "moron-magnet" or referring to others as "that special kind of stupid" puts everything in perspective. It's just too funny to let it hurt.

3. **Remember, anyone who says negative things** to you is, on some level, disturbed, so to engage with them would not be a fair fight; these people are not like you—*normal*. So how can you be on the same playing field? Just forget it.

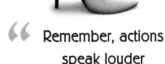

> " Remember, actions speak louder than words! "

4. **Surround yourself with people like you.**

5. **Forget the old sensibilities of the more, the merrier.** VIPs and exclusive clubs are my game!

6. **Don't buy into false pretenses and don't sell them either.** Your friendships will survive and thrive!

7. **Beware of sweet talk.** Remember, actions speak louder than words!

6

PRETTY ME

LAUREN'S LESSON:
FOOD AND OXYGEN ARE LIFE ESSENTIALS, BUT SO ARE PLATFORM SHOES, OVERSIZED SHADES, BIG HANDBAGS, AND ENORMOUS PILLOWS

It was 11:30 AM on a Sunday; I was barely awake after a late-night birthday party at the new hot spot at the Standard Hotel in the meatpacking district, the Boom Boom Room, where the drinks are seventeen bucks a pop. Nightlife in New York City is so expensive, but it does make you drink less, since to go out and actually get a buzz going could equal a small mortgage. But I was getting ready to meet my mother and Aunt Robyn (my second mom, who, like my mother, looks like a movie star) on Long Island for a day of furniture shopping for my new apartment. About four months ago, I moved into a one-bedroom apartment that I completely renovated. This included the kitchen, which had to be reconstructed for my height; I call it the Shorty Kitchen! Now I actually feel tall because I reach almost everything except the top shelves . . . but who can really reach the top shelves of anything?

At this point I still had no couch or coffee table, so I'd been confined to my baby blue bedroom. My bed had become my couch, my desk, and sometimes my coffee table. That morning, I gathered enough strength to put on leggings, a T-shirt that reached my knees, my vintage, light-brown cowboy boots (not as high as my trademark high heels, but they are two and a half inches tall), and my new black peacoat with patent leather piping along the sleeves. I headed downstairs, said good morning to the doorman, and got into my white Audi TT convertible. I love getting out of the city and seeing actual grass and breathing in fresh air. Surprisingly, there was no traffic in the city and I got through the Midtown Tunnel within minutes. However, the hope I conjured to fly on the Long Island Expressway (called the L.I.E. by most natives) proved to be a pipe dream, as once I got past the first exit I hit the brakes. Everyone was going furniture shopping with my mom and aunt apparently.

Finally, after sitting in traffic for more than

> " I love getting out of the city and seeing actual grass and breathing in fresh air. "

an hour, I arrived at Exit 50 (or Bagetelle Road), which meant only five more minutes to my parents' house. My phone rang, and my "Hello" was greeted by my mother impatiently shrieking, "Where are you?" (her favorite phrase since I was a teenager) and "Are you close?" Literally three minutes later, I arrived at the house and walked in through the garage entrance. My mother was wearing an outfit similar to mine, except hers was accessorized with black leather knee-high boots. Of course, she looked so much better in her outfit than I did, but I digress. She was waiting in the kitchen and was taking her midafternoon vitamins (think Samantha taking her vitamins in *Sex and the City 2*). She greeted me with a big kiss and hug, the way only a mother can, and I proceeded to make excuses for myself: "Ugh, I hate the L.I.E., and I am so exhausted from going out last night. Do I look terrible?" My mom, in her own subtle way, suggested, "Why don't you wash your face and put on some makeup?" Fifteen minutes later, having donned mascara and sporting a freshly cleaned face, I was out the door with Mom to meet Aunt Robyn at Peter Andrews, the antique replica store in Farmingdale.

It was so overwhelming: there were more than fifty different couches, chairs, armoires, and other types of furniture, all in different patterns, and older women coming at you with pens stuck in their hair and clipboards in hand, ready to take your order. Talk about presumptuous! My taste is comfy with a romantic feel; I like beautiful fabrics, cushy couches with big pillows, gold antique mirrors. My bedroom always has to be a little bit floral and feminine with flowers. Some of my colleagues and even some of my friends expect my home to be decorated in a modern style because that's the way I dress—yet my home decor is anything but modern. It is really pretty and homey with French Country accents. For my apartment revamp I wanted pieces that were less girly and more romantic.

" **Fashion and design are a huge part of who I am.** "

My home-designing taste comes from my mother's side of the family. My grandmother Nanny Bev was an interior decorator, and I remember seeing different swatches of fabrics and paint always lying around her house when I was a child. My mother and her sister Robyn acquired Nanny Bev's sense of home design, and our homes and even my parents' salon, Ultissima, became the brainchild of Nanny. No matter what, at one time or another, one of the women in my life was redecorating.

Coming from a long line of decorators and hairdressers, including my parents and my Nanny Bev, it's no surprise that aesthetics mean a lot to me. Fashion and design are a huge part of who I am. I like my choices in clothing and decorating to reflect my personality and attitude: positive and upbeat with a bit of sparkle. My home and clothing are a way of expressing my two sides—one is very fashion forward (expressed through clothing and shoes) and the other is very feminine and soft and earthy (expressed at home). I take great pleasure in fluffing pillows and lighting candles at home, and primping and preparing for work each day, an evening out, or a weekend away. To look good and have a clean, beautiful home makes me feel better about myself; it's a way to exhibit my accomplishments. When I walk out of my apartment, I feel confident that I am put together in a way that makes a statement about who I am, and when I am home I come to a place that makes me feel comfortable and safe to be in.

My personal fashion style has definitely been influenced by my parents. They are supertrendy and always look their best, and they taught me to take pride in my appearance because that is one way you take pride in yourself. When you are "put together," you figuratively stand taller and shout, "I feel and look good today, therefore I can conquer anything." What you wear when you have a job interview, go on a first date, meet the parents of your latest love interest, or go out with friends communicates who you are and how confident you feel.

Style has been important to me as far back as I can remember. I discovered it was a way for me to identify with and assimilate with the other kids in elementary and high school and then, ironically enough, to stand out and set myself apart in college and in adulthood. As a child, I always felt that if I dressed like the other kids I wouldn't stand out, and therefore I would be more accepted. Not to say that if you didn't wear what everyone else was wearing then you would be left out, but it was a quick fix at my young age, something I could control, and seemed logical enough to me. It's hard to say whether the fact that I wore parachute pants with scrunchy socks or appliqué T-shirts from the flea market back in '85 was actually responsible for me fitting in better with the other schoolkids, but it certainly helped me *feel* like a part of the crowd, and in adolescence, what is more important than that? But of course with age comes maturity and confidence, and once I got to college, I stopped focusing on not being liked or feeling alienated and used my fashion sense to set myself apart, both physically and emotionally.

> Embracing a personal style is also a great way to express your inner self.

I think a part of my predisposition to look the part comes from being hyperaware of the label game. You remember Chapter Two, right? Well, I believe that having your own personal style allows everyone to have a sense about you even when they don't know who you are, and that goes a long way toward combating the tendency they'll have to impose the wrong labels onto you. Personal style dictates how *you* expect people to notice and react to you. This is not to be confused with caring too much or being overly preoccupied with what other people think of you, and I definitely don't want you to glean that. However, the reality is that people are going to pass judgment, make assumptions, and so forth, and whether you like it or not, some of these people will be important in your career, your love life, and your friendships, so projecting who you are allows you to have more say in their decisions about you. It's a power play. These days, with so many people making rash assumptions about you in work, love, and friendship, any ammo you have is worthwhile.

Embracing a personal style is also a great way to express your inner self. Some people have art, poetry, or music to interpret their moods, feelings, aspirations, and personalities. Well, those of us who are not inclined to sing on Broadway can cloak ourselves with a silk scarf when feeling powerful and sophisticated, or an oversized flower pendant à la Carrie Bradshaw when we feel feminine and pretty, or a pencil skirt when we are having a skinny day. But what's also wonderful about having a personal style is that it is a personal reinforcement of who we are and who we want to be . . . to ourselves. Our garments and our home decor are as personal as the lines on our palms—an imprint of our many sides, our interests, and our depth.

As I said before, I personally use fashion to make a statement and to help me stand out. I mean, at my height, one could get lost in the crowd, and to be a wallflower is definitely not my calling in life. Besides, I come from a very creative and fashionable family and have a mother who should have been a model, as she is absolutely the most stunning woman in the world. Mom has always taught me to dress appropriately for my body. And my father, who is also very fashion-conscious and extremely direct, has always told my sisters and me what looks good on us and what doesn't.

> **When I open my closet, I feel like I'm about to enter a wonderful new world where possibilities are endless.**

Having a knack for fashion also means I am a good shopper, but I try to be a reasonable one. I'll invest in a few important pieces, classics that are well made and last, like the perfect black dress from Cynthia Rowley and an oversized black bag from Michael Kors (oh how I love Michael!). Oh, who am I kidding? I have no rhyme or reason when it comes to shopping: if I like it, I buy it, and my closet reflects that motto. When I open my closet, I feel like I'm about to enter a wonderful new world where possibilities are endless and prospects are high. I have every color T-shirt and tank top, forty work and "going out" shirts, twelve different kinds of black leggings (hey, I like to vary my textures), nine pairs of jeans, at least twenty skirts, and perhaps thirty different dresses—and that was just the last time I cleaned out my closet.

Then my accessories are a whole other beast, with costume jewelry taking center stage. I must have twenty different rings, all twice as big as my fingers, with the oversize watch to match. Thanks again, Michael Kors, for making the best watches and for styling my wrists in the past few years. I discovered large rings from one of my best friends, Juliet, who introduced me to the world of costume jewelry. (Juliet, my drawers, fingers, and my credit card thank you.) Anyway, big rings, high heels, and big pillows make me feel good. I guess the larger the item (like the higher the heels) the more in control I feel. I think that comes from the fact that I am a big person who appears small, so the bigger items feel authentic to me and more in line with who I am rather than how I appear in stature. Hmmmm, I mentioned once before that I like irony, so for a little woman I seem to like big merchandise.

Let's get to the really good part: shoes, of course—which you have already learned have such a huge impact on my life. Ladies, it's all about the shoes: the higher they are, the better I feel. I love shoes so much that I won't even let the wrong size deter me from wearing the right pair. My feet are very small—size 4—so I often have trouble finding stores that carry what is referred to as a specialty size. I've convinced myself that there is really no difference between a size 4 and a size 5, which is the smallest size you can most easily find in a shoe store. So I buy size 5 or 5½ shoes and stuff the toes with paper or cotton—that's how important heels are to me! Watch out, Cinderella!

One day I went to Steve Madden's showroom in New York City for a business meeting (I know. Tough life.), and the second I walked in I was in awe of everyone who worked there. It was like walking into shoe heaven; the smell of leather was everywhere, and every imaginable kind of shoe was within my reach. Throughout my entire meeting I could not concentrate, and I only thought about trying on every single pair and doing the shoe runway walk like everyone does when they try on a new

> " The smell of leather was everywhere, and every imaginable kind of shoe was within my reach. "

pair of shoes. It was like a dream. Then I asked the million-dollar question: "Do you carry a size 4 or a European 34?" The head of partnership looked at me and said with a sigh, "No, I am sorry. We just don't have a big demand for such a small size." My dream of walking away with new shoes was squashed. Taunted by the Steve Madden meeting, I needed a shoe fix, so I went to Nordstrom.com—my own heaven—and bought a pair of black size 4½-inch booties made by Nine West. Thank you, Nine West, for getting on the small-size bandwagon, and thank you, Nordstrom, for stocking them (even though the cotton trick will still be in my future plans. Hey, I'll take what I can get).

I've always felt as if I was walking in a hole because I am so short. My clothes were always too long, especially pants and skirts. So when I was finally old enough, around the age of seventeen, to be able to wear high heels without anyone screaming at me, I never wanted to wear anything else. They were one item I could put on to avoid having alterations done. And when I wear heels I can actually see more than my forehead in the mirror. My insistence on wearing high heels drove my doctors and physical therapist crazy, and it still does. They tell me I can't wear them or they have the look of fear in their eyes when they see me walk in—but wearing them (and wearing them well, if I do say so myself) is part of my expression of fearlessness, of who I am inside. And besides, I have perfected the art of walking in high heels. Unlike a couple of Miss Americas of late, I have yet to take a tumble while wearing mine.

My obsession got me into credit card debt, which was not so good. While still in college and on a limited budget my MO was to charge shoes from Nordstrom (and everything else) on my credit card . . . not a good idea, of course. Eventually I got out of debt—and I do not recommend indulging in shoes (or anything else, for that matter) you cannot afford. Like my parents say, "Don't spend more than you make." But shoes make me happy, so I figured out a way to balance my love for them with a more sensible approach to my finances: I look for sales and only buy two or three pairs a season. Just like watching your weight, it's not about deprivation, but moderation. I have a bigger budget today than I had while I was in college so I can afford what I want, but just because I can afford it doesn't mean I will over-pay or not look for bargains. Finding bargains is half the fun of shopping.

Looking good has always been one of my main priorities. For instance, I will buy twelve

> " I love being a girl and everything that comes with it, especially the indulgence in fashion. "

pairs of shoes before I'll spend $199 on a new pair of crutches. Fashion is so much more important than having new crutches. I've had the same crutches for five years now. And even though they are something I use every day, all day long (except when I am sleeping), I'm simply not interested in replacing them. One time, on a stylish whim, I did have couture crutches made. I wore a pink and white floral dress for my bat mitzvah, and had crutches made to match. They were spray painted white and wrapped with pink ribbon and were the talk of the party.

I have to admit that I do take care of my crutches and repair or replace them if necessary. I always have an older pair as a backup, if needed. For instance, the rubber tips (the soles of the crutches) wear out very often since I walk around a lot, so I always have a box of ten replacement crutch tips in my closet. I change them at least once a month as they get worn down. Sometimes I need major maintenance on one of the crutches; my father has become the ultimate crutch mechanic. He can fix them in a matter of minutes.

Basically, I love being a girl and everything that comes with it, especially the indulgence in fashion. I believe that is one of our biological rights as women! Plus, I am lucky enough to work in the publishing world. At Hearst Magazines, which is one of the top magazine publishers for monthly women's magazines, dressing well is encouraged. If you are wearing something hot, new, and trendy, it becomes the catalyst for great conversation, no matter if you're in a meeting, in the ladies' room, or at the amazing café in the lobby.

I know there are many women out there who don't share my enthusiasm for shopping and for adorning myself with flare in the latest trends. In fact, many women seem to lack the self-esteem to believe that they deserve to cloak themselves in pretty things or to splurge once in a while on a practical yet fashionable item. That's why I wanted so much to write this chapter: If you think *you* have body image issues, what do you think *I've* had to contend with? If I could walk into a shoe store and deal with the fact that I can't find a shoe to fit me without a special order, or find pants or a skirt that will fit my small, deformed legs, then anyone can figure it out. Throughout the years I have definitely beat the fashion blues by figuring out what looks best on me. Trust me, there are some clothes that I wish I could wear but they are not in the cards—skinny or low-waisted jeans or shorts are two examples. The skinny jeans looked weird (and so do low-waisted

> " Throughout the years I have definitely beat the fashion blues by figuring out what looks best on me. "

ones), and I never wear shorts since I hate my legs and never want to show them off. Everyone has insecurities and mine is baring my legs; therefore, I wear things that compliment my disfigured legs, like leggings, skirts, and certain types of jeans. My skirts are never too short and are always one or two inches above my knee and all my dresses come to the knee. I never wear a shirt that does not cover my butt, and when I'm at the beach in a bikini I will always have a skirt so no one can see my hips.

Look, I know I am trying to be a role model for you, so one would assume that would include telling you how beautiful you are no matter what your body type. But I'm not going to patronize you. My admission that I prefer to de-emphasize my legs or hips might sound like I am hiding them from the world and that I am not proud of my body, which might very well be true, but if doing so makes me feel better, then I believe that's all that matters. Don't you? So I say accentuate your best qualities, as all the best stylists in stores and on TV advise, which will compensate for what you don't want to show off, but don't obsess about those problem areas. *That's* where you'll get into trouble. To know and admit your downfalls, whether physical or anything else, is actually healthy in my opinion. It's a sign that you accept who you are, flaws and all. It's when you allow those flaws to deter you from living happily and fully that you get into trouble. When I put on something that is very fashionable but shows off the deformities, I tend to get insecure and will immediately throw it off and put something on that makes me look and feel great. And my point is that there is always something out there that *does* look good and makes me feel great, and I promise the same is true for you!

Too many women get so caught up in the self-examination/self-hatred game that they don't look good for the things that do fit them well and compliment them in every way. Instead they catch the "why bother" syndrome and believe they are so hopelessly fat, ugly, unpopular, broke (you fill in the blank) that they wave the white flag and say, "Why bother trying to look good? Nothing will help." Too many women are striving for perfection, and that's just not possible. They think that anything less than a perfect body or a pretty face does not deserve careful attention and grooming. I see women who I can tell, just by looking at them, are saying to themselves something like, "Well, until I lose twenty pounds, I am not going to bother trying to look good." If you look good you will actually feel good about yourself and

> **If you look good you will actually feel good about yourself and more people will be attracted to your new and improved attitude.**

more people will be attracted to your new and improved attitude.

Why does self-esteem always boil down to weight? Weight has to be one of the scariest words in a woman's vocabulary, and it's something that we all deal with on a daily basis. Watching one's weight is something that women (and an increasing number of men) have in common, but for me, it's even more challenging as I am the height of an average eight-year-old with a thirty-four-year-old appetite and palette. I have to try to stay at a consistent weight, otherwise my bones will not be able to support me, so watching what I eat is literally a matter of walking or sitting it out. (Talk about dreading the scale.) Of course, there are times when I have weighed more than less and—trust me—I do feel it. I not only feel bloated and fat but my legs begin to ache, which is the telltale sign that I must either start calorie counting or hit the gym more than usual—or both.

My current gym routine is three times a week of intense physical therapy where I concentrate more on my core and upper legs than anything else. When I was a kid, therapy consisted of just what I needed to do for it to end quickly, but today I take a much more rigorous and mindful route and push myself to break a sweat, which helps boost my metabolism. Since it's really hard for me to do cardio, I try to push myself as much as I can through therapy.

Like it is for anyone else, making myself go to the gym is the hardest part, but once I am there, I throw myself into the workout and actually start to enjoy it. Either I am walking swiftly or I am bogged down by extra weight, so I have come to perceive the gym as a necessary and healthy part of my lifestyle. I hope you can see exercise in the same way I do: not as a vanity issue but as a health issue. If you can find value in the knowledge that exercise is a way to prevent so many ailments like osteoporosis or high blood pressure (and the biggie, heart disease), going to the gym won't be solely about

> " Taking care of your health is the second nicest thing you can do for yourself. "

a competition with the elliptical machine's calorie counter (the accuracy of which I was always skeptical, anyway). It will be something you are doing for yourself beyond getting into a smaller size, and that can be very freeing! Then you can let the cycle begin: hit the gym to exercise for health, become healthier, feel better about yourself, beat the "why bother" blues, dress for success, take pride in who you are, hit the gym (happily). Taking care of your health is the second nicest thing you can do for yourself. Loving yourself is the first. So give it a go.

Pretty You.

Want to say, "Pretty Me" and mean it? Keep these tips in mind:

- Never compromise your femininity for success . . . you don't have to. You're a woman and you should express that any which way you want to. Wear what you want to wear as long as you look in the mirror and feel confident that you can take on the world—even the business world, as long as you leave the over-exposed cleavage behind.

- Remember: Just because it's in fashion doesn't mean it's for you. Always dress for your body and you will look and feel great.

- No matter what your style is, express it out loud in a fabulous way.

- Look the part you want to play in life—people will treat you like you want to be treated.

- Don't ever apologize for your personal style. Work it the right way and people will respect you.

- Exercise for health first and the body you desire will come naturally. If you shift your priorities and goals a bit, you will force a terrific new cycle of vibrancy and self-love that you never imagined could happen so naturally (thank goodness for endorphins!).

- Be fit, not fragile. Set goals like running more miles

or trying a new class like spinning or Zumba. Or if you can't run and bike (I can't) take a walk in the park with your friend, or put on your iPod and take a stroll. Pushing your endurance will give you self-confidence and lead you to have a better sense of yourself and what your body can do.

◆ Push out of your comfort zone. I started really testing my physical endurance once I hit adulthood. I was amazed at what I could do, if I just let go of the fear and self-doubt. Next time you're out to exercise, add just two more minutes to your routine, or change the incline to just one degree higher, or push that resistance level past what you always do. You will feel totally different afterward, and that glow will be infectious when you hit the town!

" I was amazed at what I could do, if I just let go of the fear and self-doubt. "

7

UNFORGETTABLE

LAUREN'S LESSON:
BEING DIFFERENT IS
A GIFT AND AN ASSET

The official definition of the word "unforgettable," according to Dictionary.com, is "impossible to forget; indelibly impressed on the memory." After I looked up "indelibly" (it means "making marks that cannot be erased, removed, or the like"), I thought about that definition. *Indelibly impressed on the memory . . .* That's me! I'm like permanent marker on the brain. When I say I'm unforgettable, I mean that in the most humble sense. It's just something that happens to me, and I like to think that peoples' affinity to remember me, either by face or by name or even by association to someone or some place, goes beyond the fact that I am "the little girl with the big voice." Okay, I realize I am not your average-looking female; I walk in stilettos, I use crutches, and I have bright red hair, so of course I will stand out more than the average woman. But I also have worked my butt off to be remembered for exuding a unique blend of confidence, attitude, and enthusiasm. I hope this combination attracts and inspires people even more than my physical stature.

But while I am hopeful, I am not naive. In reality, when we initially meet people and have fledgling relationships, we are inclined to notice their physical traits first—the color of their hair, the way they dress, or their stunning beauty (or lack thereof). This is why most employers know immediately after a job candidate enters the room whether or not they will hire him or her. It's probably

> As unique as I am on the outside, I am even more unique on the inside.

happened to you. Remember my thirty-one job interviews? Maybe you've been remembered because you have a beauty mark or pink hair or a certain swagger in your step. Or you've reinvented your look à la musicians or actors (like Madonna) who remain relevant and notable because of their look, boldness, and confidence. Whatever it is, can you imagine *only* being remembered for those qualities, day in and day out, even though you have so much more on the inside to offer? Well, it's like that for me, except ten-fold: as unique as I am on the outside, I am even more unique on the inside, so it is with a lot of effort that I strive everyday to enable my inner traits to shine through, so that not too long after meeting me, people remember me for the substantial stuff and not just the stunted growth.

Because of this goal, it's always been important to me to be unforgettable, and I want it to be for you, too. Why? Because there's no better characteristic for a woman to have than to be unforgettable. Whether in business or your personal life, being unforgettable is the first step to personal and professional success. (Remember the employer above?) The road to unforgettable is a two-step process: 1. Identify your unique qualities—the things that make you *you*, and 2. Leverage them to become your biggest assets! This has been such a predominant theme in my life that I actually had the honor to write a magazine article. The article for *Marie Claire* chronicled my efforts to parlay my differences into assets in all areas of my life. In this chapter, I'll take you on a similar (but longer) journey to illustrate how my two-step process unfolded, and give you some unconventional wisdom on how you can use what you have going for you to be unforgettable too!

But first, a little side note: unforgettable should not be confused with notorious. When I say I am unforgettable, I don't mean that I am remembered for being obnoxious and full of myself or for stealing someone's job or abusing my staff. That's notoriety. Unforgettable means you have made others react in positive ways; you embody a trait that makes them feel good about you and about themselves. You inspire them and offer them something—whether it's a shoulder to cry on, an ear to bend, or a great idea for their next ad campaign. They, in turn, want to pay it forward, and anyone who can compel another to do that is simply *unforgettable.* So, let's get to it.

Remember when I told you I sang to LL Cool J when I was just nearly a teenager, and nothing came of it? Wouldn't you know that I wound up running into him about two years ago? It had only been twenty years since I channeled my inner Whitney Houston for him. I was at a meeting at Epic Records about a new band titled The DEY and met the band's powerhouse agent, Claudine (who, by the way, is one of the loveliest women I have ever met). We were discussing her client roster and it turned out that she also happens to be LL's manager. I told her that LL used to live down the street from me and that we crossed paths in the neighborhood from time to time, giving

> " **One of my assets is that I am bold and take chances.** "

each other the neighborly wave. The following week Claudine and I had dinner. During the course of the evening, Claudine's phone rang and it was LL. She couldn't resist and asked LL if he remembered a girl who lived down the street from him in Dix Hills. Instantly, he described me to a T. I could not believe it; one of the world's great rap stars remembered me . . . after twenty years. He even remembered my humiliating performance on his patio. Claudine gave me the phone and LL and I had about a ten-minute conversation and laughed about what I had done.

What was it that made LL remember me? One of my assets is that I am bold and take chances, so I tend to think that LL was impressed by my precocious (read *blind*) ambition, and the guts it took for me to believe enough in my abilities to walk up to the house of a celebrity and sing for him unsolicited, convinced of my own star quality. I'm sure the sight of me hobbling back down his pathway on my crutches is also *indelibly* marked in his memory, but together it all made for a nice, unforgettable package.

So what is it for you? Is it the way you look, walk, dress, or the way you speak to people that truly makes you unforgettable? Or is it just something that nobody can pinpoint but people always remember about you that makes them want to be a part of your circle? That's what I like most about being unforgettable: people not only remember who I am, they actually want to become part of my life in some way. That is such a compliment and it infuriates my sisters, especially Addy, as I am the sister who everyone always remembers.

A prime example of being unforgettable landed me two of my now-closest friends, Adam and Anthony. When I was twenty-two years old, I took my first vacation from Markham/Novell after working there about six months. It was the middle of an extremely cold winter, and my friend Jill (who was on winter break from teaching) and I decided to go to South Beach in Miami for six days to enjoy a little paradise only two and half hours from New York City. I was so excited about taking a week off, drinking frozen margaritas on the beach, and most important, getting a tan.

> It was a picturesque day . . . one of six to the ultimate tan!

We landed at the Miami airport to a beautiful sunny day, and we immediately got a cab and were off to our quaint hotel on Ocean Drive. We arrived and checked into the Beacon Hotel, where I had stayed before, so I was familiar with the surroundings. We entered our room, threw down our bags, put on our bikinis, and scurried off to the beach. It was a picturesque day, and our game was on; day one of six to the ultimate tan! After sitting on the beach for nearly five hours, we decided to return to the streets of South Beach and walk around the town to shop. Suddenly, the skies betrayed us and turned shadowy and opaque; the rain came down like pellets, and we headed back to the hotel. Jill was miserable and concerned that the weather would repeat this pattern for the rest of the week.

When we arrived back to our hotel we were completely soaked. We spoke to the concierge and asked him to check out the weather forecast. To our dismay, the forecast called for a 50–60 percent chance of rain for the next three days. Ugh, what were we going to do? The concierge recommended that we head to Key West, where it hardly rains in the winter.

The next morning we were on a new excursion. We decided to ride a bus to Key West because it was the fastest and cheapest way to get down south. Before we headed out, the concierge warned us that the hotel he booked for us had two pools, one being "clothing optional." At this point we could have cared less; we were spontaneously embarking on a new adventure, and daily unwavering sunshine was almost a guarantee!

Three hours later the bus let us off in the front of the hotel, which turned out to actually be a motel, and it looked nothing like what we had imagined it would. But still, Jill and I did not care, as the sun was shining and the pool was calling our names. We checked in but our rooms were not ready, so we asked the clerk to show us the way to the two pools. He looked a bit confused; explaining the motel only had one pool. "Okay, whatever," we muttered, and were off. With bikinis back on, we headed up the outside wooden staircase to the pool. Jill found two available seats and got us some towels. We were back in business.

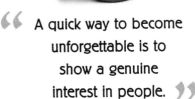

I was curious about where we were actually staying, so I decided to get up and look around while Jill napped. There were men and women with hardly any clothes on, and rows of rainbow flags blew in the breeze. Where *were* we? I immediately woke Jill up,

 A quick way to become unforgettable is to show a genuine interest in people.

and whispered, "Jill, we are not in Kansas anymore." She was annoyed with me for interrupting her sleep and told me to lie down and get some color. In response, I demanded she get up and look around. "I think we are at a gay nudist resort," I insisted. After a few more attempts on my part to get her attention, Jill finally got up and looked around. We glanced at everyone around us in astonishment. *Oh my God, did the concierge think we were a couple?*

So our vacation turned out to be a comedy

of errors of sorts, and as any unpredictable, unplanned adventure usually winds up, this vacation turned out to be one of the best I have ever had. Remember I mentioned how a prime example of being unforgettable led to meeting two of my best friends, Adam and Anthony? Although they were too fabulous to actually be staying at the run-down gay nudist resort like Jill and me, we ran into them at the pool bar. (Like us, they were conspicuous in their bathing suits.) They spotted us first because we stuck out like sore thumbs: Jill is five feet seven and tan with dark hair and eyes, and parading next to her, at four feet two with short blonde hair (the hair color choice at that moment) was me—a contrast that Adam and Anthony just couldn't help noticing. The four of us instantly connected over a martini, and ten minutes into the conversation I knew their entire life stories and was convinced that we would be lifelong friends.

I am naturally interested in people and their stories, and people remember that I like to listen to them talk about themselves. I am inquisitive and ask for more details and soak in the stories, interests, and insights of friends and strangers alike. A quick way to become unforgettable is to show a genuine interest in people, which I do all of the time.

The four of us went to shows and restaurants and did everything together for the next four days. Adam and Anthony introduced me to some of the people they'd already met; at one point I handed my crutches to Adam and went on a Vespa-like motorcycle with a man named Stuart Little and was gone for more thirty minutes. By the time we left the island everyone knew my name (basically because I told it to them). They thought Jill and I made a cute couple and asked us how long we had been together. I said "Let me put this out of the way; the concierge at our hotel booked us here, but we are not gay." The circumstances always gave people a laugh. I became the "queen" (in the straight sense of the term) of Key West. Everyone from the waiters to the drag queens on stage wanted to hang out. Because I threw caution to the wind, my experiences were full and memorable for everyone involved. Twelve years later, Jill, Anthony, Adam, and I are all still friends; and to this day we always tell anyone who asks the story of how the four of us became friends at the gay nudist resort in Key West where they weren't even staying and where Jill and I didn't even technically belong. Some things are just meant to be.

> " Because I threw caution to the wind, my experiences were full and memorable. "

I am different and I know it so, instead of hiding it, I use it to my advantage. I make myself an example of how relentless or unstoppable a person can still be, no matter what their challenges. For instance, I was recently at a business dinner discussing various projects with representatives from *Esquire* magazine and the DIY Network. As we were leaving, my colleague, Stephen, saw a woman he knew and I followed him to say hello to her. I was standing next to him as they exchanged cordialities when she interrupted Stephen and said, "Oh my God, you're the girl from the *Marie Claire* article!" She knew all about me, which is a fantastic compliment; she also said that she had seen me walk down 57th Street a few times. Now, noticing random people as they walk down the busy streets of Manhattan is a rare occurrence, but to remember them is something even more extraordinary. I suppose the latter isn't such big news considering the looks of me. But to be unforgettable means that you strike a chord in someone, and I hope that when people notice me and remember me hailing cabs while impaling the sidewalks with the rubber caps of my crutches and four-inch stilettos, I inspire them to do something unforgettable themselves. And that's one of the easiest ways for you to become unforgettable: inspire people. Be an example of someone to take a cue from, or exude qualities that others would like to exhibit themselves. You can help them do that, and there is nothing more rewarding. Every time I walk down the street, I am aware people will remember they saw a short girl walking with crutches down the street, but turning that into an asset means that while I am walking, I am also looking straight ahead with my eye on the prize, confidently owning the streets just like everybody else. It's the ambition, independence, and intention with which I walk that I want people to remember. And while I can't necessarily control what they wind up thinking or feeling, being able to know that what I am ultimately exuding goes *way* beyond the crutches is enough for me to keep pumping with my head held high. How can anyone find that forgettable? So, do the same for yourself. Next time you're feeling vulnerable, defeated, weak, or just plain forgettable, dig deep inside yourself and conjure up that magic, the fever within you that will make people look beyond what they *think* they already know about you and offer them a new dimension of yourself—beyond the surface.

> " I don't try to hide my differences or let them stop me from going out and enjoying myself. "

Another thing people remember about me is how I don't try to hide my differences or let them stop me from going out and enjoying myself. I stand out in a bar, a crowded club, or a trendy restaurant because I assert myself in a way that helps me get my unique needs met while not acting entitled. Here's an example:

A couple of weeks ago I was at Café Noir, a cute little bistro at Grand and Thompson, sitting at the bar with a friend, minding my own business. A very distinguished older black gentleman with a beard came right up to me and said, "Hi Lauren!" I knew I had seen him before, and I felt as if I did know his name, but I just could not recall it. He continued talking: "Lauren, I haven't seen you at Felix lately, how have you been?" It's true that I had not been at Felix, another favorite bistro in the city, in a while. So I just said, "Oh, I haven't had a chance to get there lately." Well, Mr. Distinguished wanted to know what I had been doing and where I had been. And we talked for several minutes before he went back to his party. All the while I was thinking, *What is his name?*

It's funny that my "friend" would remember me from Felix—it's a Manhattan hot spot that is always packed. You cannot move in there, and I either need a stool or a table so I can sit down. When a situation like that presents itself, I am the person who pushes through the crowd and makes my way to the maitre d' to tell him, "I need a place to sit." Normally, I only have to do this once; people tend to remember me and my needs. Sure, at first they remember I have "special needs," but then the fact that I am also not afraid to call attention to myself in order to fit in (how's that for a brainteaser) makes an impression on people, ultimately disengaging them and their innocent gawking, and highlighting my assertive request for a seat as an asset that they can appreciate. That assertiveness is a quality too few young women have, perhaps because they've been led to believe that assertive equals aggressive. I totally disagree; assertive means bold and confident, and those are two positive traits that will definitely put you on the road to unforgettable in any venue.

In short, I don't hide out at home thinking it would be too hard for me to contend with the hustle and bustle of the city streets, or to stand in line at a hip nightclub, or make my way up to a bar when it's blocked by unchivalrous men who are clamoring for cheap beer. I go out there and find a way to make it work for me. After enough time, that's what people like my unnamed friend ultimately remember. The same can be true for you.

> " I tend to be on the lookout for magnetic people who know how to ingrain themselves indelibly in my memory. "

When I stop and think about what I do or say that makes me unforgettable, it leads me to think about what others do that makes them unforgettable to me. We can all learn a lot from the actions of others—whether poor or positive—so I tend to be on the lookout for magnetic people who know how to ingrain themselves *indelibly* in my memory as well.

TOP TEN THINGS I FIND UNFORGETTABLE:

1. A winning smile
2. Maintaining eye contact when speaking
3. Great storytelling abilities
4. Confidence but not cockiness
5. Sense of humor, friendliness, and an engaging personality
6. Ability to find commonalities between people and relate to them because of those common features
7. Paying attention and asking questions
8. A fashion sense that stands out. If there is a story behind it, such as wearing a vintage ring, even better
9. Offering good advice and being impactful on someone
10. Refusing to be anyone but yourself!!

Overall, it is important to always show the power of your presence.

When determining what makes you unforgettable, it's important to consider what is undesirable so you can avoid those things like the plague. Here are five things I find make people *forgettable,* in case you want some guidance on what *not* to do socially (or the quickest way to become notorious):

1. Rudeness

2. Tardiness. Don't make anyone wait more than ten minutes and be sure to call

3. Being unprepared for whatever the occasion is (Do your homework!)

4. Dressing inappropriately. It's a sign that you don't care about what you are doing and could care less about the people at the event

5. Complaining. We all have our own problems, so hearing you whine about yours will prompt others' eyes to glaze over . . . and remember Charlie Brown's teacher from the *Peanuts* comic strip—"Wah-wah-waahh-wah"

" Set the example for confident living and everyone will remember your name! "

Remember, the most natural way to become unforgettable is to find those unique aspects about yourself and use them to inspire others. Set the example for confident living and everyone will remember your name!

Here are few other things to mark indelibly in your brain
when it comes to forging your own unforgettable path:

1. Don't ever let your perceived differences or faults
   keep you from going out there and busting ass!
2. Stand up and be confident in everything that you
   say or do. You can't be remembered if you speak
   only when spoken to or use apologetic tones
   when sharing ideas.
3. Use your unique voice to get a point across. Don't
   try to talk in anyone else's language; it will seem
   inauthentic and forgettable.
4. Recite a story of an incredible moment in your life.
   Anecdotes are great. If you want people to remember
   you, provide them context. They will always know
   you shared something personal about yourself
   and/or made them laugh or think because of it.
5. When you are in a business meeting, leave people
   with your favorite tips or lessons learned. If you
   share some wisdom, you will be remembered as a
   team player, with something to offer others. Even
   years later when your paths cross again in other
   business, people will remember that you showed
   them kindness in the big, bad, business world.

8

COUPLA THINGS
ABOUT COUPLING

LAUREN'S LESSON:
FINDING AND KEEPING LOVE IS
HARD ENOUGH, BUT DOING SO
WITH INSECURITIES IS IMPOSSIBLE

There is an old New York saying that goes something like this: It's easier to get hit by a bus then to find love in a city of more than eight million people. On second thought, I'm not sure it's as much a saying as it is a cruel rumor. Is it true? I would have to say that it very well could be, as the inability to find a decent man is something my girlfriends and I have lamented over so many times. We are all looking for the passion, the connection, the sign, the sweep-me-off-my-feet moment that has only been experienced by Cinderella and her other Disney cohorts (but even *Cinderella* had to pay her dues). And I'm no exception. I was the girl who never had long-term relationships but wanted to love and be loved so badly. My life with men has been extremely unsatisfying and something that is really hard for me to discuss, but that's because this issue is so emotionally charged for me—as I suspect it is for you—because so much of our self-worth and self-image is wrapped up in who loves us, when, for how long, and how well. And in my case, it seemed that no one was loving me, at least not in *that* way, so clearly I needed to find alternative ways to feed my soul and build my self-worth. I also needed to learn that while finding love is important, it's not *the* most important thing. Loving yourself is the most important thing. And once I learned that, I needed to discover what else is important to me and accept my life for the amazing gift it is. And as I will reveal throughout this chapter, a funny thing happens when you find acceptance . . . but first let me even the playing field by sharing some of my not so proud love-life moments, in the event you're not feeling as high on love as everyone else around you.

> **It was like I was their freeway to love.**

From junior high through college, I was the "just one of the guys" girl who had the humiliating task of setting up men I was interested in with my girlfriends. It was like I was their freeway to love: call or hang out with Lauren, and ask her to put a good word in for you with that cutie she hangs out with in homeroom. It took me a little longer than I wished it would have to catch onto this lousy game. Looking back, it's enough to make me vomit. Needless to say, I was never the hot girl popular boys wanted to date, and that became a matter of contention for me from the time I was twelve.

When it came time for school dances, or the slow dance at a bar mitzvah began, or the air was threatened by the sounds of a cheesy power ballad at a Sweet 16, my heart raced, convincing me it would soon stop (and in those moments a death wish was not completely out of the question, aside from the wish of a giant boulder plopping right in front of me in the school gym so that I could either hide behind it or crawl underneath it). I would think to myself, *None of these boys will ask me to dance.* I was right every time, so I would save face by heading outside and hanging out with the smokers, even though I didn't smoke. Time after time, I would hope and pray that things would be different, but they never changed. I finally resigned myself to the fact that I'd spend my entire life being the girl who doodled hearts around the names of secret crushes. The problem was that in my dreams, we lived happily ever after, while in real life I was the girl who was waiting to be kissed for the first time.

As I grew older and put myself out there more, my insecurities surrounding my disability skyrocketed because I knew that was the main reason I didn't have a boyfriend. There might have been other reasons too, but I was always positive that my disability was reason number one. And it's not like it was a situation you'd see in an '80s teen flick, where the girl goes on a diet, gets her braces removed, puts some straightener in her hair, and transforms to become captain of the cheerleading squad. My genetic disorder wasn't going to be removed by a fairy godmother or by trading private tutoring for popularity! I am sure by now you get that I don't do powerless and helpless well, so the idea that I had no control over what I could do to join the ranks of the paired-up club really hurt and dismayed me. And as if I wasn't already convinced by the end of high school that I was destined for spinsterhood, senior prom put the final nail in the coffin.

> " My genetic disorder wasn't going to be removed by a fairy godmother or by trading private tutoring for popularity! "

Prom: One of the biggest events in a girl's life. I knew what I wanted to wear, who was going to be in my limo, and where the prom after-party would be held in the Hamptons. The only thing that was missing was my prom date. I remember the sleepless nights of anxiously wondering if anyone would ask me, or if I was going to have to bite the bullet and ask someone myself. All of friends were asked, so here I was, the last one. Finally, bullet-bitten, I asked a friend, but no grandiose romantic interludes were in order as we were "just friends."

Don't get me wrong: I did eventually graduate to having the occasional boyfriend and "hooking up" with men, but no one wanted to commit. And when I was at my lowest, I would think, *And who can blame them? I'm short, walk with crutches, and have a rare genetic disorder. Not necessarily something to plaster all over Match.com or JDate.com.* I became frustrated because while these are the superficial things that are most unforgettable about me, there are so many other things I have to offer, and I was afraid I would never get the chance to give to someone special. So what did I do? Enter self-pity mode.

Now, I am writing this chapter because I know we all love a good pity party, with the party becoming a real headliner when it revolves around an unrequited love, loss of love, or lack of love. I have been there in more ways than you can imagine (I spilled some of it earlier) and I want to help spare you the depression dance. I also want to help you avoid the rut that we can get ourselves into when we can't distinguish the important difference between our love life and our *life*. And that *is* an important difference.

So, are you down on your love luck? Here's what I want

you to do. Think about your life as it is without a boyfriend. Hell, even if you have a boyfriend you can complete this exercise. (Who knows, maybe you'll dump him afterward.) What aspects of your life would be enhanced by having a boyfriend? For instance, would having a boyfriend nail you that promotion? Would having a boyfriend calm the waters between you and a feuding friend or relative? Would having a boyfriend make you like your thighs, make your butt slimmer, or help you pay off your Amex bill? Okay, so unless you are deluding yourself, the answers to these questions (with the exception of a temporary *yes* to the thighs and butt questions—only because at first he'll tell you how much he likes them), is a big fat *NO*.

> " What aspects of your life would be enhanced by having a boyfriend? "

Now, I understand that this is still no consolation, but what you should remember is that all of these things and so much more encompass your *life*. And life is for living, not for playing sappy songs to. What happens during our proverbial pity party is we allow ourselves to sabotage our lives so they match the underlying emotions that we experience in our love lives (or lack thereof). *Stop* doing that! It took me awhile to understand that who I am is not wrapped up in the arms of a guy. When I came to that realization, I started to focus on the things in life that really mattered to me, like the issues we've discussed in the chapters of this book: being a good friend, not stooping to other people's levels, avoiding the label game, becoming unforgettable, focusing on personal style, learning to communicate better and more effectively at work, traveling, health and vitality, and family.

Next, I want you to think about why you want a boyfriend in the first place, and whether you want to have a boyfriend just for the sake of having one. Been there, done that. It's what I call "The Dinner for Three Syndrome." It's kissing cousins to the "third wheel." According to the UrbanDictionary.com, a third wheel is one who deters the socialization of a couple, perhaps when being invited out of pity or through a sense of duty. He or she is called the third wheel because "having any odd number of wheels on an object generally messes it up." Both the Dinner-for-Three Syndrome and the third wheel can put enough pressure on a girl that she will actually go out and date just about anybody, just for the sake of rounding up to an even number.

I was the third wheel so many times that I had to get my tire changed. Dinner for three? How humiliating! When I was with friends who swore they never minded, I was the one who felt awkward and intrusive. My favorite was when the waiter would look at our table for three and ask, "Will there be one more tonight?"

It wasn't until I was in my early- to mid-twenties that my third-wheel status began to bother me the most. My three closest friends, Jill, Jason, and Juliet, were always dating someone, and since we would hang out all the time, I was constantly the extra who would attend dinner, a movie, or whatever. The dinners would always be fun, but what I hated was the public affection—a brief kiss, holding hands . . . totally benign stuff—but it was in those moments that I felt alone and despondent and especially wistful for someone with whom I could be affectionate.

Even worse than the public affection was when the couple would begin to fight and look to me for my opinion. I wasn't there to referee. Half the time I didn't know why I *was* there. The worst was making judgment calls between Jason and his girlfriends. Since we were ten, Jason's behavior has always been slightly erratic, but in a funny way. Because I shared the same number of X chromosomes with his girlfriends, who became frustrated or confused by said behavior, I was put in an automatically biased position—against Jason! Bad move. Then,

> " Who I am is not wrapped up in the arms of a guy. "

of course, the fight would be over and they'd go home together while I accompanied myself home. Not sure which is worse: sitting through an entire dinner with a couple, getting in your car alone at the end of the evening, or, in my case, being the first of the three people the cabby drops off because you are alone.

But in all suffering there is wisdom, and what I learned about being the third wheel was that I was really ready to connect and couple, to be a part of someone's life and allow them to be part of mine. Here's a little tip from the trenches that I hope will help you save face and avoid many solo cab rides home: If you must engage in a third-wheel dinner, make it more of a social gathering then an intimate dinner for three. If that's impossible to do, then when you accept the dinner invitation, please accept it with the foresight that you may feel a little blue while there, and know how you are going to combat those feelings. If you know that you can't take it and will turn the evening into an existential crisis with every kiss or intimate moment you'll witness, then don't accept. It's not fair to your friends, and it's not fair to you to show up with a feeling of self-pity or harrowing guilt.

Now, if you are up for it, here's a little trick: Be mindful of the conversation and keep it steered in your direction. Don't take over and be single-minded about it, but make sure you find relevance in their topics and stay away from being involved in their cute banter or whimsical love stories. Sure, you're interested, but maybe your interest can only last through the appetizer.

So what happens when your three-wheel vehicle finally flips over? When your friends break up or have been single for a while, the prowl begins. The easiest way to "hook up" or find a potential man is go out to a bar, and an invitation to head out and meet people was, for me, like Christmas coming early. I loved going out high with the anticipation that I could possibly find my prince that evening, so I was always the first one in.

But many times the second cousin of third wheel and Dinner-for-Three Syndrome would show up uninvited, and her name was Wing-woman. Have you ever been the wing-woman? It's happened to me several times in my life. I'd get all dressed up in something sexy to go out for drinks or dancing, and my girl-friend would get hit on and I wouldn't, so I'd sit at the bar and order another drink (or five). At some point, the guy that my friend was talking to might come over and say hello to me so my friend would think he was gallant. Needless to say, when the night unravels like that, it's a bust and you go home feeling worse than ever.

> " Dealing with the enigmatic world of dating and mating can make you crazy. "

Dealing with the enigmatic world of dating and mating can make you crazy. When it's going well, you can feel invincible, beautiful, whole. When you are in a slump, like I was in my role of third wheel or wing-woman, well . . . you question everything you do, try to change everything about who you are, and sometimes you do some not-so-wise things. The number one no-no? You settle.

Am I a seeker of true love and commitment or just settling for like or lust? As I stayed loyal to the dating scene, this was a question I asked myself constantly to keep myself and my priorities in check. Even with all the Dinners for Three or single New Year's Eves I endured over the years, nothing made me feel as lonely or confused as when I settled for someone just for the sake of having someone. And by asking myself this type of question, just checking in on what Lauren really felt and wanted, I helped myself identify when I was settling and when I was going after what I felt I deserved and wanted.

When I reflected on the reasons I settled and I took an informal poll of my friends about the times they've settled, I identified some overlapping reasons why we are sometimes guilty of doing this.

1. When we settle, we are reacting to a sense of urgency. Either we feel threatened by time, by conditions, or by expectations. In essence, we panic and feel the need to Band-Aid the situation or mask it with a

bogus relationship.

2. We are trying to fill a void. Hey, loneliness is a strong emotion and, biologically speaking, loneliness exists to warn our very social species to find someone and couple up . . . the fate of the species depends on it!

3. We are cracking under peer pressure. One more night as wing-woman and you'll be sure to call Nurse Nan (from *One Flew Over the Cuckoo's Nest)* yourself and ask for a room reservation!

" **By settling, you are giving away your power and selling yourself short.** "

4. We are selling ourselves a bill of goods that subconsciously we know is worth zilch.

5. Our insecurities have gotten the best of us. Clearly we aren't worth more than the situation or person we are settling for. *If he likes me, that's better than nothing.* As if we don't have choices . . .

By settling, you are giving away your power and selling yourself short. I did this, and for all the reasons I stated above, but the last reason listed was a biggie for me. I was convinced the reason I could not meet a man who I would care about and who would care about me was because of my disease. Back in high school, I would fear being alone for the rest of my life, fear that I would never to be given the opportunity to show another person how much I had inside of me. As I got older, this fear intensified and threatened to turn into a prophesy. There was nothing I could do about my physical condition, which made me even more sensitive to the idea that I was destined to be alone. *What if this is it? What if I will be alone for the rest of my life?* I couldn't accept that. I decided it was time for the big guns: online dating. But I was soon to learn that was only going to add fuel to the fire.

I signed up for JDate.com and was encouraged by the number of eligible men who could want a respectable, intelligent, twenty-four-year-old woman who was climbing the ladder of career success. And that's how I described myself. Did I ever think about putting forth on my profile that I walked with crutches? No, because that is not how I see myself. As I sat down to write a personal profile, literally the first things that popped into my head were the things that I allow to define me. As I've explained earlier in this book, McCune-Albright, my height, and my crutches were the things that *labeled* me. I wanted to be *defined* by my personality and who I have become as a woman. I believed that if I included *walking with crutches* in my profile, I would automatically be categorized as handicapped—and that would be all any man would be able to think about. I was not denying my handicap, but on those dating sites there is so little room for redemption, so I thought I'd take my chances and give people the other things to consider about me.

However (and not surprisingly), reminiscent of the second interviews I got called on (when the employer would be surprised by my stature) men were so taken aback by my disability that they would get angry because I never mentioned it before we met. One guy in particular was so mean to me after what I had considered to be a good date; despite the fact that we ended our date kissing, he wrote me an e-mail the next day about how beautiful, smart, and fun he thought I was, but that he could never date a woman who was as short as I was and walked with crutches. (This, coming from a man who disclosed during our date that he had had two hip replacements to help him walk better.) There it was! The proof I had been waiting for: that it indeed was my disability that would keep me alone for the rest of my life. This devastated me to such a degree

" The most important thing I learned was not to be afraid. "

that I began having anxiety attacks. I immediately took myself offline and decided that dating and the fixation to couple up was not going to cause me any more anxiety. My insecurities had finally gotten the best of me, my prophesy had been fulfilled, and it was either going to be downhill from there or I was going to live the rest of my life—solo or not—as the happy and secure woman I was meant to be. I wasn't exactly sure how to go about doing that, so I did what any self-respecting New Yorker would do—I went into therapy.

What I found through therapy was acceptance. Acceptance for the things I cannot change. Acceptance for the fact that I cannot control what men think of me. And acceptance for the powerlessness I have over certain situations. What I figured out was you cannot find love (or anything else in life) unless you truly believe its going to happen and you accept the person you are. If a man cannot accept you for who you are, then you are fighting a losing battle and he isn't worth a second look. You have to decide how you want to spend your time and what you want to focus your energies on—the lost cause? Or yourself? The most important thing I learned was to not be afraid, and I decided that whether it would take me one year or thirty to find someone, that was fine by me. I love myself, and I knew that when I eventually found love it would be true and kind.

After I finally accepted that I was by myself, I became happier and free. I acted more like who I really was and I wasn't preoccupied with the questions that I had no control over answering, like *Why didn't he ask me out?* Or *Does he think I'm pretty?* Or *Will he call?* I used to do that a lot. And after a while I realized that all those times when I was assessing the scenario between a prospective date and me, I would never ask myself what *I* thought of *him*. Whether he was up to snuff or if I thought he was interesting or funny enough to be with me weren't factors in my decision to date him. It was all about the approval I was seeking *from him*. Well, accepting my single status, which led me to like myself a whole lot more than before, enabled me to quit this pattern of thinking and find acceptance in the facts that: 1. I would be fine with waiting for my destiny; 2. I would be the one who called the shots; 3. I'd trust in the time it would take for all this to happen.

> " Just when you ease into a nice, comfortable life for yourself, the gods of acceptance look down on you and laugh. "

And as I mentioned earlier in this chapter, a funny thing happens when you find acceptance. Just when you think you have it down pat, when you ease into a nice, comfortable life for yourself, the gods of acceptance look down on you and laugh: *Hey, Lauren's got it together. Let's muck it up. Let's send her . . . love. Clearly, she's ready for it.* And then it happened, and in the most wonderfully ironic place—on a staircase.

It was November 17, 2008, and a colleague of mine had invited me to the opening of his new Broadway show, *American Buffalo,* featuring John Leguizamo. I invited my friend Cameron to accompany me to the show and the after-party. As we climbed the stairs to the amazing roof deck at 230 Fifth, the venue for the after-party, this sexy Latin man with curly brown hair and deep chocolate eyes was behind me, and he tapped me on the shoulder. At first I thought he was being polite and just wanted to excuse himself so he could pass me, but instead he said matter-of-factly, "I think you are beautiful. Would you like to have a cocktail with me?" I was absolutely stunned and thrilled at the same time.

We continued up the remaining few steps and the three of us sat at the bar and drank festive hot apple cider with rum. His name was Nelson and we spoke for hours. Cameron noticed that the two of us were hitting it off and he decided to go home. I felt so comfortable and natural and I wasn't overthinking. I just felt that this man immediately saw me for who I was; he even saw me at my most vulnerable—climbing up one step, one crutch at time up a flight of stairs, and still asked me out. He called the next day to ask me out on an official date. No three-day rule, no games.

Nelson and I have been together since, and we recently began living together in my new apartment. Living together brings a whole host of new insecurities, which are less about wondering or worrying what he thinks about me and more about finding and establishing the true intimacy that makes living with someone fun and rewarding. Living together shatters any chance in hell that Nelson might never find out about the habits, the nuances, the pet peeves, and everything else that makes me *me*, and the same goes for him. We now know everything about each other (which was a huge leap of faith for me), and we accept each other for who we are. He knows that sometimes I need help, and he always goes the extra mile to be the one to support me.

> **My victories never came easily, but they were so much sweeter in the end.**

Falling in love was scary. I wanted to trust Nelson and trust in our connection and his intentions, but when you bring your insecurities from the past, as well as your fears that your prior bad experiences might repeat themselves, it's hard to throw yourself in. But I did it anyway. I felt I deserved to take the risk. I accepted that I couldn't control whether it would all end in heartache, but I could control whether or not there would be an opportunity for heartache. All my life I put myself out there: insisting to my doctors at the tender age of five that I wouldn't need a wheelchair; singing outside a famous rapper's house; defending myself to a faulty advisory board at a sleepaway camp; taking several unpaid and inconvenient internships; moving on from rejection after rejection thirty-one times to get my first job offer. All of the experiences in my life had led me to this moment. I thought it was only logical to believe that the same success would come to me in love as it had in all the other aspects of my life. My victories never came easily, but they were so much sweeter in the end. I don't know at this moment if Nelson and I will live happily-ever-after for the next fifty years, but as I said earlier, I have accepted me for me and have found a love to treasure every day. Whatever comes next is not in my control, but I am up for whatever does come. Remember that for yourself. You have got to *try* in everything you do. I'd rather live a life failing at everything I try than to never try at all.

WHEN GRAPPLING WITH THE COMPLEXITIES OF COUPLING, REMEMBER THESE IMPORTANT POINTS:

1. Don't fear being alone. It's definitely better to be alone than to be with someone with whom you do not truly belong.

2. You are not that girl in the gymnasium. Let go of past insecurities. If you take them with you

on the road to love, you will fail at love every time. I had to move on from Lauren, the "friend," and Lauren, the girl without a dance partner at the school dance. If I can do it, so can you.

3. Settling is for cowards. If you have dated someone in the past just to prove something to yourself or others, or for any of the other reasons that I noted earlier in this chapter, forgive yourself and move on. But please don't do it again. Settling for someone is a betrayal to yourself.

> " Owning up to your discontent will help you feel dignified in the end. "

4. Don't have a pity party, play the victim, or judge yourself by the number of "winks" you receive on a website.

Your energy can be spent elsewhere— like on being the best you possible!

5. Be honest with your friends and yourself concerning your feelings about being single. If you are feeling like the third wheel or are tired of being the wing-woman, say so. Owning up to your discontent will help you feel dignified in the end. Nobody likes doing things

that feel inauthentic, so nobody can blame you for wanting to stop.

6. Come to terms that you might be alone. Once you stop fearing singlehood, you can get so much accomplished . . . like getting to know yourself, spending quality time with yourself, and learning what is really important to you. Being alone is a great opportunity for introspection. When you come out the other side, you'll love yourself for it and be ready for others to love you.

7. Accept. Just do it. It feels good to relinquish control.

8. When you do meet prospective dates, remember: they should be trying to pass *your* test, not the other way around. Don't forget your priorities or requirements. You are not a piece of meat he's inspecting. Check in with yourself as he's chatting you up. Is he *your* type? Do *you* like *his* smile? Are you interested in what he's talking about? Don't worry about what he thinks about you. That's a determination you have no control over.

9. Trust. Just trust in yourself, in others, in the process of the crazy conundrums that come your way. You can handle the good, the bad, and the ugly, so let go of the fear and let it all happen. You deserve to at least try.

EPILOGUE

An unexamined life is not worth living

—SOCRATES

It has been nothing less than a pleasure to write this book, and it's truly my gift to the world: all I ever want is for you to go after your goals and live a long and happy life. Of course, this must be done in the greatest stilettos you can find!

But the tricky things about writing a memoir like mine is identifying your milestone moments, putting them under a microscope, and finding the wisdom in them to share with others. I took this task very seriously, and I was not prepared for the roller-coaster ride an examined life can be. The discoveries I made while interviewing my parents about the dark days of my diagnosis took quite a hit on me emotionally, as I was only a small child at the time and did not remember much of it. Hearing the details of the daily ins and outs took me to a dark place in my mind and in my heart, because it was *my* life. When I sat down to write about the details, the emotions poured out of me. To know and understand the pain that I personally went through as well as the emotions my parents had at this time was unconscionable. I would sit on my bed in my apartment, close my eyes, and try to picture myself—at the doctor's office, in pain, trying to understand what was happening to me. I could picture myself staring at my parents, wanting them to have all the answers—but they didn't, and neither did the doctor. When I was diagnosed my parents were younger than I am now; my God, they were just young adults themselves, who never imagined something like this could happen to them. To hear them describe the emotions they went through broke my heart, and I would wonder, *Did they ques-*

> " As hard as you may think it will be, take a look at your life, examine it, and make yours a life worth living. "

tion why this was happening to them or to me? Were they disappointed that their first child had a disease no one could really understand and grasp? Of course, when I posed these questions to them, their answers were that they loved me and that love was all that mattered, but I still had a hard time grasping that notion.

As I was writing on my laptop, I would sometimes stop and begin to cry, because my life today seems so different from the way it was back then. Today, I am an accomplished adult who loves her life and is happy to live, breathe, and walk every day. Perhaps I *am* so happy today because subconsciously I know what it's like to live through hard times, and I never want to go back there. The feelings that came to me were overwhelming, feelings that I'd never felt before; perhaps I'd bottled them up as a child because I never wanted to return to that sad place.

But, I did somehow find the courage to go back in order to head forward, and I see my life and those who have shared in it through a totally new lens. It's like meeting myself for the first time, and I hope this book will inspire the same for you. As hard as you may think it will be, take a look at your life, examine it, and make yours a life worth living.

This year of writing has been the most exciting and emotional one I have had in a long time. I learned so much about myself and discovered an emotional side I never really knew about. I was always a force to be reckoned with, and I never let my disease get to me, but learning and truly understanding has given me the strength to want to know and understand more. My great desire is to truly educate everyone around the world that when God throws you a lemon, you can make sweet and tasty lemonade. Life is to be lived large, and now that I have gained additional knowledge and tremendous feelings, I am ready for the next chapter of my life to begin. I have the perfect pair of stilettos picked out!

ACKNOWLEDGMENTS

There are so many people who have had a huge effect on my life and who make me feel like the luckiest woman in the world. All of you have contributed to making *Unstoppable in Stilettos* a reality.

Above all, I thank my parents, Holly and George, who taught me to never stop believing in myself as I seek to achieve my dreams. Your belief in me, combined with your strength, positivity, and love, made me the woman I am today! This book is my dedication to how much I love you! And thanks to Ultissima for always making me feel pretty!

To my sisters, Addy and Emily, who have grown into my best friends; your guidance, laughter, trust, and sensibilities have always kept me on my course, which emotionally allowed me to write this book. P.S.—thanks for letting me in your closets for the past twenty-five–plus years!

Aunt Robyn, you've been there through everything and have always made me laugh, dressed me like a diva, and taught me the "real" lessons that a girl must know—which in turn have turned into some of the great lessons that I am offering in the this book! Jenna and Jesse, who are more like sisters than cousins: Thank you for being there for so many of the wonderful stories that I discuss in the book. Jenna, a huge kiss and hug to you for working at Michael Kors and keeping my feet as happy as they can be.

Carolyn, you truly have been the greatest gift in my life. You challenged me from the time I was five years old, which allowed me to showcase my strength and passion. Also, you will always be the voice in my head that tells me to stop hopping!

A very special thank-you to my editor at HCI, Michele Matrisciani, who believed in me and my story from the day the amazing Ross Ellis sent my proposal to her. Without your energy and passion, this book could not have been published. You have really helped me write and mold this book into something that I am truly proud to present to the world.

Jason, you're not only my best friend but like a brother, and someone whose strength in life is absolutely terrifying. When I need to be cheered up or put in my place, you're the one I know who can offer me a kind word . . . wink wink. Plus, since you're always going to act like you're fifteen, I know you will keep me young.

Juliet, we've known each other for more than twenty-nine years, and I have learned so much from you. Above all, you have taught me to live my dreams. No matter how close or how far we live from each other, you will always be in my heart.

Cameron (aka "Sherpa"), in the past six years you have kept me on my path, introduced me to the country, and has shown me more amazing times in life than I could ever expect.

Mikey, what can I say but that you're my partner in crime, and so many of the amazing stories referenced in this book would not have been possible if you were not by my side. Adam and Anthony, from the day we met I knew that we would be together forever. You've become my extended family, and your two amazing children, Frances and Zachary, have offered me such joy and inspiration while writing this book.

An extra special thank-you to Jill, whose friendship over the past twenty years has been so special to me. Your positive spirit has gotten me through some of the hardest times in my life, many of which are described in the pages of this book.

Two huge kisses to Joanna Coles and Lucy Kaylin for giving me my first opportunity as a writer. Your talent and passion for your careers are something that I strive for every day.

To my amazing boyfriend, Nelson, who showed me real love for the first time in my life. Your love, affection, and tolerance of my behavior during the writing of this book are things I will never forget.

A special thank-you to John Loughlin, who helped me create the perfect job. Thank you for teaching me and for your dedication in allowing me to creatively soar though the publishing industry, and for your support as I wrote this book.

And a warm thank-you to everyone at Hearst for your brilliance in helping me to be *Unstoppable in Stilettos*.

To the rest of the Ruotolos, Monahans, and Miltons: you are the best family a person could ask for. Aunt Barbara, your eight kisses remind me that traditions never die, and if we are strong enough we can get through anything.

To everyone who helped me along the way, I dedicate this book to you and hope it brings enthusiasm, strength, and passion to everyone who reads it.

ABOUT THE AUTHOR

Photo by Nelson Aguirre Photography

Lauren Ruotolo is the director of entertainment promotions at Hearst Magazines in New York City, where she is responsible for developing strategic key partnerships with television and cable networks, music labels, and movie studios. She recently helped produce E!'s Style Network show about the inner workings at *Marie Claire* fashion magazine and is working on two one-hour specials with Scripps Networks for *Esquire* and *Food Network Magazine.* Lauren joined Hearst Magazines from *TV Guide* magazine, where she was the director of consumer marketing and promotions and created the first-ever newsstand promotion in the United States with a CD on the cover.

Ruotolo's first-person essay "Get Shorty," which shared her philosophies on living with the rare genetic disorder McCune-Albright syndrome, was published in *Marie Claire* magazine in 2009 and was one of the most responded-to articles in the magazine's history. Ruotolo is on the advisory board of GlamourGals Foundation, Inc., Love Our Children USA, and is an active member in the New York chapter of Women in Communications.

Visit Lauren on Facebook, follow her on Twitter (Lauren jaenyc), or log on to www.unstoppableinstilettos.com and www.laurenruotolo.com.